THE KISS OF INTIMACY

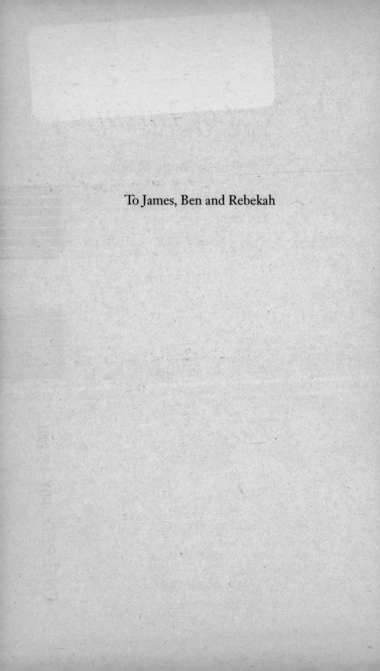

To James, Ben and Rebekah

The Kiss of Intimacy

Reflections on the Song of Songs

ANDY AND JANE FITZ-GIBBON

MONARCH
Crowborough

Unless otherwise indicated,
biblical quotations are from the
New Revised Standard Version, 1989

British Library Cataloguing-in-Publication Data.
A catalogue record for this book is available
from the British Library.

ISBN 1 85424 321 7

Produced by Bookprint Creative Services
P.O. Box 827, BN21 3YJ, England for
MONARCH PUBLICATIONS
Broadway House, The Broadway
Crowborough, E. Sussex, TN6 1HQ.
Printed in Great Britain.

CONTENTS

FOREWORD

For many Christians, 1994 proved to be a year of unforgettable encounters with the love of God, as times of spiritual refreshing broke out upon our land. Supernatural love in new and overwhelming measure began to be poured into our hearts by the Holy Spirit (Rom 5:5). Paul's prayer for the Ephesians was fulfilled among us with a new immediacy. We not only continue to meditate upon God's all surpassing love, but we are also coming to know in living encounter this love that surpasses human understanding (Eph 3:14–21).

We have feasted upon the goodness of the love of heaven (Is 55:2), tasting and seeing that the Lord is good indeed (Ps 34:8). The Spirit of adoption has been testifying to our spirits with a new eloquence that we are indeed the children of the living God (Rom 8:15–16). The felt Christ of whom believers often testified in the Great Awakening, the intimate testimony of divine love in the believer's inner being, has become again a living and vital witness of love. Some who have known little of the touch of God for years, perhaps not since the first excitement of the time of their conversion, have come alive to Christ again. Others who have kept in step with the Spirit over the years have enjoyed new opportunities to go still deeper into God. As he pours his love into us, our first love for Christ bursts newly into bloom.

We have seen this love reach the places no one else could

reach, not only in our own lives, but in the lives of those who have been bruised and wounded by rejection and love deprivation. When the love of God besieges the human heart, the Spirit of God begins to melt in moments the defensive barriers that would take hours of counselling to overcome. That does not mean that we abandon longer term counselling, but such patient care now takes place alongside the most amazing experiences of supernatural love therapy.

What's more, many couples have enjoyed the 'honeymoon effect'. After the first meeting where Claire and I experienced the refreshing together, we drove home with a heightened sense of love for one another. Throughout these months, as I have spoken and prayed at conferences and churches, I have seen the honeymoon effect touch many couples unmistakably. I prayed for one couple recently who sank to the floor under the presence of the Holy Spirit, her head gently nestling upon his supportive arm. When they finally got up to go home, they were as attentive to one another as a couple who have just fallen in love for the first time.

So is all this no more than mere self-indulgence? Is it indulgent when lovers enjoy nothing more than one another's company? Is it a weakness for the newly married to want to be alone together? Still less is it out of place for believers to enjoy the 'kiss of God', for surely the intimate outpouring of the Holy Spirit is nothing less than this.

In previous times of renewal and revival, the Song of Solomon has often returned to centre stage. The Cinderella of Old Testament books, so often passed over and neglected, becomes afresh a source of inspiration, helping us to comprehend the burning intensity of divine love. I am so grateful to Andy and Jane Fitz-Gibbon for calling our generation back to this book. Their meditations are full of a profound and moving glimpses into the love of Christ for his bride. Out of their own experience of the outpouring of the Holy Spirit, and their thoughtful mediations upon the unchanging Word of God, they have come to a depth of insight that is rich and rare.

Andy and Jane are also a couple whose love for one another has deepened and grown richer with the passing of years. As you read this book you will learn more not only of the love of God, but also of Christian love in marriage. The divine love has overflowed to strengthen their relationship together, even as their marital love has overflowed, not only to their own children and in pastoral care for others, but also in a ministry that is absolutely vital in the modern world, providing foster care for children from less fortunate homes.

This book has been an inspiration to me, as a Christian, a husband and a father. My prayer is that it will lead many others into a deeper intimacy with the glorious Lover, crucified and risen, eternal and divine.

Rob Warner
April 1995

———————

To clarify the structure of the Song of Songs, when passages are quoted at length the sections spoken by the girl are in *italics*, while the sections spoken by the shepherd are in roman type.

PREFACE

Some years will always be remembered as significant, sometimes for good reasons, sometimes for bad. 1994 will be remembered by many Christians as a momentous year. In the goodness of God there was an outpouring of the Holy Spirit which impacted many thousands of lives.

A few were eagerly expecting a new move of God in fulfilment of prophecies. We suspect that most, like us, were blissfully unaware that anything was 'afoot'. Yet not quite 'blissfully'. We had been in pastoral ministry for thirteen years and were somewhat dry. Like many others we had passed through the 'stages' of charismatic renewal and had seen God work in amazing ways in the lives of people. But 1994 found us dry, somewhat confused and all but burnt out. In the latter part of the year God surprised us. His blessing came unexpectedly, suddenly, and was profound in its impact, both upon us and our closest friends.

Whenever there is a move of God, there will always be those who bring a criticism of it. One such criticism of God's blessing in 1994 (usually from those who had merely heard about the 'goings-on' or who had briefly touched it) was that it was all noise, laughter and with little substance. Our experience, on the contrary, was that beyond the physical manifestations, of which there were many, was a deep heart work of God in many people. God was restoring the spiritual passion of his people. Many fell headlong in love with Jesus

Christ as they soaked in the presence of God.

We were no exception. We laughed, fell down, wept, shook, convulsed, jerked and saw visions with the rest. It was exciting, heady stuff. To the onlooker it may have appeared somewhat bizarre . . . would God really put people through that?

On the 'inside' our testimony is that God has done a profound work of grace. In our lives and in the lives of our children and friends we have seen the transforming power of God.

As we write there is no 'let-up' in what God began in 1994. The refreshing at Toronto, Ontario, Canada is one year old today. We have shared in nightly renewal meetings at Sunderland, Tyne and Wear, England for 24 weeks.

God's work continues . . .

For us, part of the fruit of this refreshing has been a new intimacy with God. We have spent, over the months, much time in the Song of Songs, finding again Jesus as our first love.

We are very aware of the shortcomings of our work. We know for sure it is not the last word on the Song. We have ourselves been greatly blessed in considering the fruit of earlier renewal movements and their work on the 'Song of Love'. However, we offer this small book as testimony to the fruit of the recent refreshing.

Our sincere prayer is that the Father would lead us all into a passionate love for his Son . . . indeed, that the love he has would be ours, that we might find our truest delight in the Lord Jesus Christ.

Andy and Jane Fitz-Gibbon
Stocksfield, 20th January 1995.

INTRODUCTION

An abandonment, a holy recklessness, is awakening in the spirits of God's people. The Spirit of God is calling us forth, taking the truths of time and eternity and using them to awaken us out of complacency. Before the world comes to an end, God will raise up a church full of people who are hungering for God-centred Christianity. The denomination label won't matter. If the Son of God is being ministered in power, and his personal beauty and loveliness are unveiled, people will flock to him.[1]

I believe that in the years to come the Lord will release more revelation of himself through the Song of Songs, the ravished song of the beloved for his Bride.[2]

The prompting from God to write this book came to Andy during a delicious day by beautiful Cayuga Lake in the Finger Lakes region of New York. Friends are a wonderful gift from God and we are privileged to have good friends on both sides of the Atlantic. On this particular day Andy was enjoying a day alone with God at a lakeside house provided by our good friend Zetta Sprole. He had determined to spend the time reading, praying and thinking through various issues before the Lord. The sky was cloudless and the September sun was warm with the temperature in the 80's. There was an occasional cooling breeze and, somehow, the presence of God matched the day. God was overwhelming! It was the kind of day we never want to end, for God was speaking clearly and powerfully after an arid period of almost three years.

In May of 1994 God had drawn our attention to Psalm 63:

> O God, you are my God, I seek you,
> my soul thirsts for you; my flesh faints for you,
> as in a dry and weary land
> where there is no water.

It had become the cry of our hearts. We had known the excitement and joy of God's presence many times and longed to know again the soothing warmth of the Spirit. On many occasions over the years we had experienced the joyous surprise when God speaks personally to our hearts. We did not know it at the time but the same psalm was being given to many in the United Kingdom as God prepared to refresh the church with an outpouring of life-giving water that none of us were prepared for, or even dared dream of. It has since become evident that many in leadership in God's church had, over the last few years, become dry. In the dryness God had been preparing us to receive a new movement of the Spirit.

Andy's day on Cayuga Lake came three weeks into our family's entering the blessing God was sending upon the church in many parts of the world. In January 1994 God had begun to refresh the church in the most remarkable way. Beginning in Toronto, Ontario a tidal wave of the Spirit, power and love of God swept through many churches of all denominations in a relatively short time. We were privileged to receive God's refreshing. It came upon us unexpectedly and in ways we had never imagined.

For us, as for many, part of God's refreshing was to read Mike Bickle's book *Passion for Jesus*, in which Mike opens eloquently and passionately the need for a deeper relationship with Jesus for all God's people. His prophecy that God would bring more revelation from the Song of Songs echoed in our own hearts. On a number of occasions God has brought us back to this beautiful book to rediscover him as our lover. During one period Andy had preached through the book and it became something of an oasis, both for him and those who received the ministry. Some years down the road it still stands as one of the sweetest points in his time as a pastor.

Swimming in the warm waters of Cayuga Lake, with God caressing his soul as the water caressed his body, it was as if God laid the whole project before him. 'Andy, it's time to immerse yourself again in my love. The Song is to become again your guide book, your resting place, and the chamber of love where you will find me.'

Subsequently, during a time of resting in God's presence at the Airport Vineyard in Toronto, a clear word was given with regard to a joint ministry for us both. Part of that word was that we were to 'model intimacy'. A strange word! But we took it to mean that God was going to draw us into a greater personal intimacy with himself and that, as a couple, we were to model an intimacy of relationship which would reflect in a small way the love between Christ and his church.

One of the blessings that we have observed in other couples who have been deeply touched by God in the present refreshing is that they have been drawn closer together. At one meeting, during a 'say-hello-to-someone-you-don't-know' time, we turned to see an older couple (perhaps in their seventies) who were entwined in a beautiful and loving embrace. Andy commented, 'You two look very much in love!' 'Oh, we are, we are, God is so good!', came the reply. It is as if we are touching something close to the heart of God.

It is that closeness to God's heart which is revealed in the Song of Songs.

The heart of the Song

The Song has caused not a little controversy. It was forbidden for Jews to read it until they were thirty years old. Others have questioned whether it should be in the Bible at all, for the simple reason that it never mentions God! For this reason alone, there seems to have been some dispute as to the place of the poem within the canon of Scripture. But there have always been those, in both Judaism and Christianity, who have viewed the book as a picture of the relationship between God and his people, Yahweh and Israel, Christ and the church, or Christ and the individual believer. Dr Martyn Lloyd Jones said of it that it is 'a mine of spiritual treasure and one of the most exquisite expositions of the relationship between the believer and his Lord to be found anywhere in the Bible'[3] That's quite a commendation!

We have always had a fascination with the Song. Early in our Christian lives we were both drawn to Watchman Nee's interpretation[4] and were greatly helped. (We have two much thumbed-through copies dated 1974!) His teaching rooted us in a Christianity which was of the heart and which sought to be captivated and conquered by God's love. Interestingly, whenever there is an outpouring of the Spirit it seems that God's people are drawn like a magnet to the Song. In the outpouring of the Spirit in the early part of this century, for instance, Jesse Penn-Lewis wrote a marvellous interpretation,[5] as did Hudson Taylor.[6] Many of these older commentaries are excellent. It does seem, however, that in each new move, with subsequent generations, God gives new light, more insight and makes the Song of amazing relevance.

The Song of Songs expresses for us more completely than any other part of Scripture both God's longing for our love and the outpouring of the divine heart, to the point of overwhelming us. There is no doctrine here, other than that Christ loved the church and gave himself for her. There is no formula; no 'how to do it in easy lessons'. There is only God revealing the lover's heart and being poured into the depths of the believer's heart. A Jewish commentator wrote: 'the whole world is not worth the day on which the Song of Songs was given to Israel. . . . the Song of Songs is the Holy of Holies.'[7]

Interpreting the Song

There are many ways of interpreting the Song. It is at one level a book of poetry comprising a number of 'snapshots' of love, with apparently little connection between them. In these terms, it stands as one of the great pieces of literature on the universal theme of love. Because it is in the Scriptures, we may take it as God's great affirmation of human sexuality. In fact, one commentary on the Song sees it as a book offering advice to newly married (and not so newly married!) couples.[8] In this way it is a book which is somewhat explicit in affirming the beauty of erotic marital love.

There is something here for Christians to learn who have, sadly, imbibed and been raised on an understanding of sexuality which sees it as in some way wrong or dirty. The Song of Songs might help us reclaim sexuality from its post-Augustinian misinterpretations, its Victorian prudishness and its post-1960s flippancy and degradation. God designed marital love as a thing of beauty and holiness. The Song demonstrates that for us.

Yet this beautiful love poem has usually been understood as dealing with more than the wonders of marital intimacy. It is taken as in some way allegorical or typical, finding in human love a reflection of the love of Yahweh for Israel or Christ for his people.

While there is no explicit reference in the Scriptures, both Old and New Testaments, to the Song (it is never mentioned or quoted from), allusions to its central theme are found many times.

Isaiah 54:6: For the LORD has called you like a wife forsaken and grieved in spirit, like the wife of a man's youth when she is cast off, says your God.

Isaiah 62:5: For as a young man marries a young woman, so shall your builder marry you, and as the bridegroom rejoices over the bride, so shall your God rejoice over you.

Jeremiah 2:2: Go and proclaim in the hearing of Jerusalem, Thus says the LORD: I remember the devotion of your youth, your love as a bride, how you followed me in the wilderness, in a land not sown.

Ezekiel 16:32: Adulterous wife; who receives strangers instead of her husband!

Hosea 2:19–20: And I will take you for my wife forever; I will take you for my wife in righteousness and in justice, in steadfast love, and in mercy. I will take you for my wife in faithfulness; and you shall know the LORD.

John 3:29: He who has the bride is the bridegroom. The friend of the bridegroom, who stands and hears him, rejoices greatly at the bridegroom's voice. For this reason my joy has been fulfilled.

Ephesians 5:23: For the husband is the head of the wife just as Christ is the head of the church, the body of which he is the Saviour.

Revelation 19:7: Let us rejoice and exult and give him the glory, for the marriage of the Lamb has come, and his bride has made herself ready.

Revelation 21:2: And I saw the holy city, the new Jerusalem, coming down out of heaven from God, prepared as a bride adorned for her husband.

Revelation 21:9: Then one of the seven angels who had the seven bowls full of the seven last plagues came and said to me, 'Come, I will show you the bride, the wife of the Lamb.'

Revelation 22:17: The Spirit and the bride say, 'Come.' And let everyone who hears say, 'Come.' And let everyone who is thirsty come. Let anyone who wishes take the water of life as a gift.

So, then, while the Song does not mention God, and though there are no explicit references to the Song being allegorical in other scriptures, we are well justified in believing that the reason for its inclusion in the canon of Scripture is, like all other books, for our learning. As the Spirit gives insight and our hearts are drawn in love towards Jesus, we will find much in the Song to stir our spirits and fill us with thankfulness.

In the nature of things, there will be many differing interpretations and explanations for the Song at this 'mystical' level of understanding, and not one of the interpretations will be adequate on its own to explain the depths of the book. We are looking at the unfathomable love of God! The longer time we spend with the book, the more will be revealed. Because we are dealing with a relationship – that of believer and Saviour – any attempt will be somewhat subjective. We are looking into the believer's heart and finding there the revelation of the heart of God.

Andy is grateful that his father led him to Christ when he was fifteen years old. Though in his latter years we lived a long distance from Laurie Fitz-Gibbon, whenever father and son spoke on the phone Dad would ask 'Son, are you still reading the word? It's the most important thing for you.' He instilled within him a love for the Scriptures. Andy's father was a dispensationalist in the school of E.W. Bullinger, who believed in 'rightly dividing the word of truth' in a particular way through a meticulous study of the Bible. It was a noble and studious way, but one which we began to find inadequate and, in time, we learned to plough a different furrow into the wonders of the Bible. Bullinger's *Companion Bible*[9] is, however, a monument to careful scholarship. He was a formidable scholar of biblical languages and produced more in his lifetime than most of us would dream of – and all without microchips and word processors! It is Bullinger's basic outline for the Song which we are following here. A similar interpretation is given in *The Amplified Bible*,[10] though at certain points there are differences. It is an interpretation which, like all others on the Song, is open to criticism, but is one which has blessed us in our reading and understanding of this wonderful book.[11]

An overview of the story

How then are we to apply this poem? How are we to typify it?

In presenting a spiritual interpretation of the Song, there are two methods we could use, somewhat closely linked but with a slightly different emphasis. To *allegorise* the story would be to find in every phrase of the poem some spiritual meaning, usually linked to a text elsewhere in Scripture. To take the story as a *type* would be to take the general sweep of the story or each particular scene within it, rather than the details. It is the latter of these two interpretative methods which we have chosen to follow, though not exclusively! From time to time we fall into allegory where there is a very clear warrant from the New Testament.

It is all too easy to take an allegory and look at all the details and provide a spiritualisation of every part, giving a spiritual meaning for every phrase in the poem. If we attempt to do that, we may turn up some great insights. We might also let our imagination run riot and lead us down a few blind alleys! In general, we should not attempt to form doctrine from an allegory, but need to look for clear teaching in other parts of Scripture, most particularly the New Testament. Some allegorisations are very clear. Some are somewhat more vague.

Here are a few examples. In 7:2 the shepherd lover says, 'Your navel is a rounded bowl that never lacks mixed wine.' In medieval times this was interpreted as referring to the communion chalice. It's doubtful that we would want to take it that way today. In 4:1 the shepherd says, 'Your eyes are doves behind your veil'. Now we might allegorise that in this way: 'Ah, that must be a reference to the Holy Spirit who is a dove . . . so it must be speaking of spiritual eyes . . . the eyes of her heart have been enlightened by the Spirit'. Now that might be acceptable for we know that the Spirit is like a dove in other parts of Scripture.

But then how about 'your teeth are like a flock of sheep.' We might allegorise: 'Teeth are used for eating. Not one of these 'sheep' is barren . . . so the Shulammite must be good at eating. This is an allegory so it must refer to spiritual eating. Therefore she reads her Bible every day . . . It points to the value of a daily quiet time!'

We might find ourselves in all kinds of difficulties this way. The above example might 'prove' a spiritual lesson, but it takes little imagination to realise where it could lead astray.

To see the story as typical would be to see the shepherd as the Lord Jesus Christ, lover of his people, and the Shulammite as the believer who the shepherd lavishes his love upon. But the course of true love does not run smoothly! There is that which encroaches upon their love and which seeks to destroy it. Solomon, who might be the world, the believer's own corrupt nature, or the deceiver, tries to win her through enticement and flattery. There are periods of separation and darkness in which the believer's heart longs for her lover. There are even periods where the beloved will not stir herself for her lover. Love is tested, at times to the limit, but is in the end triumphant. It is the wonderful story of the triumph of God's love for all those who believe – illustrating perfectly Paul's revelation that 'nothing shall separate us from the love of God'.

The poem is taken as a very touching love story between a beautiful girl from Shunem (or Shulem, hence Shulammite) and her rustic shepherd lover. They are to be married, but one day while the girl is out in the nut garden the King, Solomon, sees her. Immediately, he is besotted with her and has her taken to his royal tents. While in the tents the other court women look down upon this poor country girl. Solomon in his turn tries to win her love by flattery and by the promise of riches. The Shulammite however is already in love. She thinks constantly about her shepherd lover; she remembers the times they have had together and she dreams about him. The shepherd lover in his turn meets with the Shulammite when he can and seeks her return with him to the country. After successive attempts to win her, Solomon realises the depth of her love and the purity of her love for the shepherd and she is allowed to marry her beloved shepherd. Their love subsequently grows and matures and the story ends with the lover and beloved renewing their vows of love for one another. A very touching story . . . Hollywood couldn't produce a better one!

There are, of course, other spiritual interpretations. The most popular one is that it is the story of love between Solomon and the Shulammite, in which Solomon is a type of Christ. Our reasons for discarding this, perhaps more popular view, are twofold. First, from an analysis of the poem itself, our 'telling of the story' seems to fit best most of the incidents. For instance, there are more allusions in the story which are pastoral, rather than royal or courtly. We will look at these in detail as we go along. (It might be useful, both before proceeding and during reading the rest of this book, to familiarise yourself with the analysis provided at Appendix A.)

All interpretation uses to some extent what has been termed the 'hermeneutical circle'. In brief, this suggests that in any interpretation we arrive at the text with a certain presupposition or set of assumptions about the text. The text is then looked at in the light of those assumptions, which in turn are modified or strengthened. The process continues as we look again at the text with our amended assumptions and interpret again, once more having our assumption challenged or changed as we proceed. Having worked with the book, meditated upon it, taught it in a congregational setting and prayed for revelation, we present our reflections to you as those making most sense to us. We are not, however, claiming any exclusive authority for the interpretation or saying that others are not equally valid.

Secondly, if we are to take the story in any sense as an allegory of Christ and the believer, then Solomon in his marital relationships was not a suitable type for Christ. Solomon was far from pure in his love. He loved the women of idolatry and was brought down by them. His lust led him captive to sin. Now, surely, that is not the kind of morality and infidelity that we want to hold up as an example of the love of Christ for God's people. Christ's love is a pure love, unmixed and totally faithful.

In the story we have two men seeking the love of the Shulammite; the one a pure love, the love of the shepherd, and the other a love (perhaps more of a lust) that would make her simply one among the thousand already in the harem, a new toy to be played with until another is found. If we are to find Christ, it is in the pure love of the shepherd.

In general terms, the story is an extended illustration of the love of God for people. It is a passionate love. There are wonderful scenes of longing, of consummation, of parting and being joined together again. We will find that it is more likely to be the general sweep of each part of the Song that is relevant, rather than each detail. So in chapter 4 with the detailed, loving description of the girl, we might want to say that the Lord Jesus Christ speaks his love for the believer; that he delights in his love; that his words of love are so intimate and without any shame. We might further want to apply that revelation through prayer and seeking the voice of Jesus as he ministers his words of love to our spirit. But more of that later!

We love because he first loved us

When Andy began to preach through the Song some years ago, the main thrust he received was contained in the words of Jesus to Peter in John 21:15 'Simon Son of John do you love me?' At that time it presented an immense challenge: 'Andy, Jane do you love me?' There was a realisation of the poverty of our love for Christ and it produced much self-examination, inner searching, and longing to be 'more committed'.

We tried to imagine what Peter must have felt. It was not too long since he had denied the Lord and turned his back on him. And yet here he was – face to face, eyeball to eyeball with Jesus who says, 'Do you love me?' What a question! It's likely that there would have been some shame, some deep-felt sorrow in Peter's heart. It was probably too painful for him to look into Jesus' eyes. We also wondered whether Peter would have wanted to simply throw his arms around Jesus and weep. Who knows? For ourselves, we would have to say 'Lord, you know we love you . . . But Lord we know that our love is not always constant, that too often it is cold . . . and Lord to our shame that we have flirted with other lovers, others have sought our affection . . . ' Many who shared that time of ministry were deeply affected and wanted Jesus to be their first love, their best love, the One in whom they delighted.

At points during the preaching series we were aware of the Song's emphasis on the shepherd's love for his beloved, but it was not too clear, not too overwhelming. We were schooled in Evangelical teaching and while we have always assented to God's love for the world, the emphasis of much of our preaching has centred on human sin, God's judgement of it, our guilt because of failing God, and God's forgiveness. Talk of grace has been present, but its effect has been to look more closely at the human side of things rather than the divine.

A great deal of preaching by many good preachers has been to try to stir God's people to do more, to be better, to get committed and to pursue holiness. The end result has been, more often than not, a dose of guilt followed by a more ardent striving for a few weeks, followed by a slipping back to lukewarmness (with more guilt at having failed remaining slightly below the surface!). We have even thought from time to time that Evangelicals/Charismatics *like* feeling guilty. More people mutter 'Good word, pastor' when you have scorched them than when you have soothed them! It has become part of Christian culture.

Even spending time with the Song was to concentrate on our love or lack of love rather than on *his* overwhelming love. More recently God has been bringing to the church new revelation of himself as the ravished lover of the church. God is not desiring our work, our striving, or our guilt for failing him. God wants to immerse us in his unending, unfathomable, unchanging love. John's wisdom, 'We love because he first loved us', has new potency and power for the believer engulfed in God's love.

Set me as a seal on your heart

We want to finish this introduction with what we believe is the punchline of the Song, found in chapter 8:6–7:

> Set me as a seal upon your heart, as a seal upon your arm; for love is strong as death, passion fierce as the grave. Its flashes are flashes of

fire, a raging flame. Many waters cannot quench love, neither can floods drown it. If one offered for love all the wealth of his house, it would be utterly scorned.

We take this as the punchline partly because it summarises the theme of the book – undying, passionate love between the shepherd and his beloved against all the odds.

In these two verses there is, on the one hand, the affirmation and sealing of love between this girl and her shepherd lover. On the other hand there is the comment that Solomon with all his wealth, and all his retinue could not buy the love of this young girl. He had tried to win this poor girl over by his wealth. Her answer to that is to utterly despise it. She will not be bought, for there is nothing to compare with the love of the shepherd.

It seems clear that there is that which all the time is trying to buy us, all the time seeking to turn us away from the love of our Saviour. The world glistens and beckons. A number of times in the Song, Solomon tries to win the girl over by enticement and flattery. He says to the girl 'We will make you ornaments of gold, studs with silver . . . ' (1:11). High flattery indeed! Satan said to the Lord 'All these I will give you, if you will fall down and worship me.' It has ever been that way.

In the Song the girl overcame the attractions of Solomon through one thing alone; the passionate love of her shepherd lover. His love was so strong that all else, even the wealth of Solomon, paled as insignificant and as mere trifles. May God overwhelm us with such love. Before you read any further it might help to pray this prayer:

Lord Jesus, reveal such love to me – such impassioned, overwhelming love – that I will scorn the flattery of the world; that all else will be as nothing compared to the passion and fire of your love in my heart.

Notes

[1] Mike Bickle, *Passion for Jesus*, (Creation House Publishers: Florida, 1993), British edition, (Kingsway: Eastbourne, 1994), p 102.

[2] *Ibid*, p 134.

[3] Note was made of this quote from Dr. Lloyd Jones some time in the past, but not from where it had been taken. If anyone knows the quote and could tell us where it is from, we would be grateful.

[4] Watchman Nee, *The Song of Songs*, (CLC: Alresford, 1965), first published Taiwan Gospel Bookroom, 1954.

[5] Jesse Penn-Lewis, *Thy Hidden Ones*, (The Overcomer Literature Trust: Poole), n.d.

[6] Hudson Taylor, *Union and Communion*, (Overseas Missionary Fellowship: London, 1894), last reprinted 1970.

[7] Quoted in Ulrich Simon, 'Song of Songs', R.J. Coggins and J.L. Holden, *A Dictionary of Biblical Interpretation*, (SCM: London, 1990).

[8] S. Craig Glickman, *A Song for Lovers*, (InterVarsity Press: Downers Grove, 1976).

[9] *The Companion Bible*, (Samuel Bagster and Sons Ltd.: London, 1964).

[10] *The Amplified Bible*, The Lockman Foundation, (Zondervan: Grand Rapids, 1965).

[11] See Appendix B for further information on the interpretative method we have used.

CHAPTER 1

LONGING FOR INTIMACY

'Let him kiss me,' she cries! She has known the Father's kiss of
reconciliation when she fled to his feet as a prodigal child. But this is
more. This is the cry of the soul for the most intimate communion
and fellowship with the Father and the Son that is conceivable.

Jesse Penn-Lewis

Close to the heart of God is the divine longing for intimacy
with his creatures. The early chapters of Genesis give us a
wonderful enactment of the divine order; a beautiful garden
in which the Godhead places the first human being. There is
pictured for us unbroken communion between the human
and the divine. The portrait is not, however, complete until
God provides for the first human being the intimacy of fellowship with another human being. From the one comes the
two and the two are one flesh. The completed picture is that
of community; firstly within the Godhead ('let us make
humankind in our image', 1:26), then between God and people, and then among people themselves ('It is not good that
the man should be alone.').

The great tragedy of history is that the perfect community was broken. People, through their wilfulness, broke
their communion with God, pictured most clearly in the
story of the disobedience in the garden. There follows
swiftly the breaking of their communion with each other in
the story of Cain and Abel.

The community of the Godhead, Father, Son and Spirit,

remained intact. Yet even that, at the moment of dereliction on the cross, 'My God, my God why have you forsaken me?' was broken on account of the wilful rebellion of human beings. God's order of community was shattered through human rebellion. God's plan for intimacy was broken by human sin.

We know, however, in God's sovereign plan, that community was to be restored. In the most mysterious and deep transaction of all, when Christ died, and the community of Father and Son was broken as he carried human sin, community began to be restored. Paul's great revelation concerning Jew and Gentile, whose enmity symbolises the breakdown of human community, was that the two had become one *through the cross* (Ephesians 2:16). That terrible, yet temporary, break in the perfect community of the Godhead opened the way for a restoration of human community. Intimacy between people is restored through the death of Jesus. The truth that 'the man should not be alone' is realised only finally through Christ.

Much could be said about God's plan for restoring human community in Jesus. It is certainly a message we need to hear. There is an intense longing in the human psyche for deep and meaningful interaction with others. God made us that way; sin spoiled us; Jesus is restoring us. All that is necessary has been done to return us to that state pictured in the garden. The community of the Godhead in fellowship with people joined together in Christ is a present possibility.

The kiss of intimacy with God

However, this book is not a book about the church. We are primarily concerned with our personal intimacy with the Godhead. Through the same great transaction on the cross God has reconciled us to himself and longs for us to relate intimately, revealing his heart and leading us in his ways.

But we have only glimpsed the possibilities; we have only tasted that which may be ours in God.

Evangelists have long used the image of the 'God-shaped-gap', a place for God which is found deep in everyone's heart. It is a place which only God can fill and yet which we try to satisfy through many and varied ways. Coming to Christ for salvation is the beginning of meeting that longing, but it is only the introduction to a deeper filling. There are ever more depths to which God would take us. And the Song is our guidebook as we long for a deeper intimacy with God.

At the time of writing we have been married for almost nineteen years. We courted for about two years before marriage . . . twenty one years altogether. But we still remember our first kiss. We worked close to one another (Jane at a dental clinic and Andy at a bank), attended the same church and often had lunch together. One lunch time we were trying to cross a busy road and we held hands as we dodged the traffic. It sounds trite to say so, but the joining of hands in the simple task of crossing a busy main road was an electric moment. It was more than the joining of hands. It was, for us, the beginnings of intimacy.

We began to see one another more often, and one evening as we waited in a shop doorway for a bus to arrive we were drawn closer to one another . . . protecting one another against the cold. As our faces came closer together our cheeks touched and then finally, and inevitably, our lips met and we kissed for the first time. It was the kiss of lovers. The bus arrived, Jane boarded and Andy flew home! He's convinced to this day that his feet didn't touch the ground. There is something profound in two human beings, in love with one another, bringing their lips together in a kiss. It is a point of intimacy, sadly somewhat cheapened in our society, but nevertheless signifying a depth of closeness.

A kiss in this way is the *direct and personal expression of love*. Of course, we don't say to our lover, 'Darling, may I have a direct and personal expression of your love for me . . . ' But that is what the lover's kiss is. At this point in the story the Shulammite is in the tents of Solomon and away from her beloved shepherd. She is presently denied that direct and personal expression of love. Having tasted it once, she longs for it again.

We do not just kiss anybody in the way the Shulammite longs for. There are, of course, many different kinds of kisses. In some cultures, there is the idea of the formal kiss, often on one or both cheeks. But it is not the kiss of lovers' intimacy. There is also the affectionate kiss between parents and children, brothers and sisters and close friends. In the Scriptures there is the kiss of Judas to point out the Saviour to those who were his enemies. There is the kiss of friendship between David and Jonathan. There is the father's kiss when the prodigal returns. However, none of these are the intimate lover's kisses of the Song.

But we can see an analogy of our relationship with God in the different kinds of kisses (except the kiss of Judas!) In, for example, the story of the prodigal son, the father's kiss symbolises for us that deeply personal moment when we are embraced by God at the point of conversion. It is that first realisation that God loves us irrespective of what we have done or where we have been. It is the touch of unconditional love and the release of forgiveness, but the kiss at the beginning of the Song is a different kiss. It is a touch of God which comes later in Christian experience. If the father's kiss to the returning son expresses for us something of the beginning of knowing God, then the lover's kiss of the Song is the deepening of love, the going further, the yet more that awaits us all in our relationship with God.

The beginning of the Song, then, expresses for us this longing for such a depth of intimacy. It is not the formal kiss, nor the affectionate kiss, nor the parental kiss, but the deep lover's kiss with all its associations of intimacy, vulnerability and oneness. Such is the soul's longing after God that only the deepest of human relationships can be used as a true picture of it. But we are running ahead! Let's look closely at the Song.

The longing of her heart for more

The poem opens in the middle of a narrative which is already developing. Like much good literature we enter a story half way through, having to use our imagination to piece together that which has gone before. We are given clues later in the book as to how the girl arrived at her longing for the lover's kisses. In the outline we are following, there are primarily six scenes, beginning with the shepherd and beloved apart, and ending with a depth of maturity to their married love. In between there is the ebb and flow of coming together and separation, coming together and separation.

The story opens, then, with a scene in which the Shulammite has been taken into Solomon's royal palaces. In a later scene (6:11–12), reflecting on her love for the shepherd, she intimates that she was merely walking in the nut garden when Solomon saw her and wanted her for himself. She had not planned to be with the king, for she was spoken for by another.

The Song begins with the girl having been taken to Solomon's palace, yet still longing for her beloved shepherd. Her separation from him was a forced separation and she longs to be with him again. It begins with the desire of the Shulammite towards her beloved shepherd. The scene is set in the tents of Solomon where she has been taken.

> Let him kiss me with the kisses of his mouth!
> For your love is better than wine,
> your anointing oils are fragrant,
> your name is perfume poured out;
> therefore the maidens love you.
> Draw me after you, let us make haste.
> The king has brought me into his chambers.
> We will exult and rejoice in you;
> we will extol your love more than wine;

Song 1:2–4

There is here the clear desire for the shepherd to come and take her back with him. As she longs for the shepherd to take her home there is the sense that if only he would, she would gladly follow. She does not appreciate being in the place she is; the memory of the shepherd's love is too strong. She longs to be with him again and to experience his love. In verse 4b the sense is '*Though* the king has brought me into his chambers we will be glad and rejoice in you [ie the shepherd]'. Even here, in all the splendour of Solomon's court, she longs for the one she loves. The likelihood is that this young girl was now surrounded with more material well-being than she could ever have imagined. The king himself had fallen in love with her and desired to shower her with his wealth. But, for her, love had come and the material things of life had become utterly unimportant.

The picture is in many ways a tragic one. Having known the true love of the shepherd, she will not be satisfied with the love of the king. Her heart has been conquered by another.

Going ever deeper

The Song of Songs is a book for believers. As such, it is not particularly an evangelistic book. It is a book which speaks to the hearts of those who have already found the pure love of the shepherd, the Lord Jesus Christ. It does not start at the beginning; there is no 'ABC' of salvation. There is no teaching about the elements of the faith. It is for those who have known him and wish to know him deeper.

Strangely, perhaps, it begins in a time of separation. The love that was once vibrant and immediate is no longer there. The beloved is separated from her lover and longs for him. It speaks to us of the believer who has known Jesus for some time and yet for whom Christian life has lost its immediacy. The joy and sheer blessedness of conversion, the wonder at the Scriptures as they come alive for the first time, discovering the riches of God's love and forgiveness . . . somehow, all have lost the edge they once had. It is not to say that the believer is backsliding or walking away from God. There is no suggestion of living in sin. It is merely a slight growing cold, a place where longing for more is a prominent experience.

The Christians of a little while look at new converts and see within them the simplicity and joy which once they had themselves. It stirs in them a longing to know it again. And yet it is a longing for a deeper intimacy, a kind of holy restlessness which will not be satisfied with anything less than more of God.

For some years we have been convinced that the secret of Christian growth is in the desires of the heart. More than anything else we need a deep hunger for him that looks and longs for more and more. If we are looking for New Testament teaching of this we need look no further than the beginning of the Sermon on the Mount in Matthew 5:6: 'Blessed are those who hunger and thirst for righteousness, for they shall be filled.' There is our New Testament truth that is demonstrated for us here in the Song. To know his love more and more, and to love him more and more. Our heart cry needs to be: 'More of Christ! More of Christ! Give men a heart burning with desire for him.'

The great enemy of the kingdom of God is apathy among the people of God. The general boredom of God's people is the most effective tool the devil uses. 'Been there, done that, bought the T-shirt' shapes the life of many Christians at present. To be honest, that kind of apathy and boredom characterises many of our lives, it certainly did ours. We had seen in the past 'outbreaks' of the power of God. It lasted, usually, for only a short time. We had seen people saved, occasional healings, and demons manifesting and cast out. People had, from time to time, fallen under the power of the Spirit. For one brief period in 1990 we knew a foretaste of revival. It lasted only three weeks. Our appetite was awakened. We had also done the round of Christian conferences where talk was impressive, yet true spiritual power often lacking. Much was promised and little delivered. Simply speaking we had grown weary.

When the refreshing wind of the Spirit began to blow through the North East of England in the Summer and Autumn of 1994, we have to confess that our attitude was less than good. Jane recalls the feeling 'Is this just another band wagon to jump on for a while?' But somewhere in us was a restlessness with the present and a deep desire to know more of God. We touched the refreshing of God with hearts only a little filled with hope, yet desiring 'the more' the Scriptures had always promised. Within a few days we were aware that God was moving in a way we had never experienced before. The foretastes of the past, coupled with the periods of dryness and weariness, had been a preparation for the further outpouring of God's goodness and love.

In the purposes of God, things begin to change when spirits become restless and stir towards God. When the mundane and ordinary will no longer satisfy; and when the believing heart aches for more of Jesus, God answers his people. For all of us who have been found by him, we will never be satisfied with anything less than the love of God.

As we receive and appreciate his love there is this inner manifestation or revelation to the believing soul. It is simply the case that this inner communion with Christ is the most precious thing that we can know in this life. It flows out of his love for us and is linked with our love for him.

It is likely that if you have been drawn to read these words you have a heart for God. To the question: 'Am I a lover of Christ?', your heart response is positive. But you will have other questions. It is not sufficient for you to have become a Christian, to have experienced the amount of growth you have to date, to display a certain love for God. Your questions are: 'Lord, how deep is my love? Can I add to my love for you? Is there a deeper expression of *your* love that *you* would bring to me?' Indeed, as we read the Song it becomes clear that the beloved grows in love as she responds to the love poured out upon her. She loves because she is first loved. She has tasted the sweetness of her lover and responds with a sweetness of her own. The more she receives the more she is able to give.

Falling in love again

In her longing the beloved explains why it is there is such depth to her desire. She has fallen in love with one who has blinded her to all others. For her the saying is true 'love is blind' in that in the brilliance of love she can see nothing else which matches it. Struggling for words she compares her lover to the best of wine and the choicest of perfumed oils. She has tasted him; been intoxicated with his scent. Other tastes and other odours cannot compare with her lover. Those who are in love know that even the smell of their lover has an undefinable something which is to them most precious.

There is about love something that is above the rational. We observed some years ago a dear friend who, in his early 50s, fell in love. His first wife had tragically died following a long and debilitating illness. When we first met his new acquaintance, we realised that they were smitten. In middle age our sober rational friend had become like a little child, delighting in every aspect of his spouse to be. To try to talk rationally about their relationship became impossible. There is something about love which transcends the rational. Love defies reasoned description, which is why the most 'sensible' writings about love tend towards the poetic.

It has to do with sense. We can walk into a room full of people and have a sense of the atmosphere. The atmosphere may be warm and welcoming or cold and forbidding. We have no reason to say that; just a sense we have. When we love someone, we catch a glimpse of their eyes or their smile or even something about them which we cannot put our finger on, and we sense their love for us, there is something intangible between us and yet, at the same time, something very concrete. It is the sense of love. Certainly, in the Song, this young girl senses that in her beloved shepherd. She even phrases her longing in the language of sense: 'your anointing oils are fragrant', 'perfume poured out'. There is just something about her lover that makes her long for him; some sense of him which has overwhelmed her and which she knows deep inside herself.

It is to be the same in the spiritual realm. There is to be this longing for, this sensing after, the Lord Jesus Christ. If you have once tasted his goodness and sensed his lovely and indefinable presence deep in your soul, then you know what we mean. And the believing heart longs for more of that. More of the fragrance of Jesus within us. More of his lovely ointment poured forth deep inside us.

Draw me after you

The longing of the Shulammite is in two directions. It is first a longing for the shepherd himself. She desires his loving presence more than anything else. But then her longing moves in another direction. It is a longing to be led away from all other things. In verse 4 she says 'Draw me after you, let us make haste'. She is inviting her lover to lead her away from everything else. This, too, is the longing of love. For the Shulammite it was to be led away from the tents of Solomon and back to the country where their love could be completed and consummated in marriage.

In the spiritual realm our longing is to be led away from every distraction to Christ. We need to be weaned from the world and its vain attractions; weaned from the seeking after worldly pleasure and gratification. It is not to say that the world of culture is all bad. We are not wanting to assert the dualism of the gnostics which permeated much of the early church. It is not that material things are wrong in themselves and only spiritual things good. But because of inner corruption it is so very easy for us to worship the good gifts of God and miss God himself. The Song is our guide to fall in love with the giver of all good things, God himself.

In Christian circles there is often talk of 'giving up things for God'. Give up your hobbies, give up your desires, give up your own ways, give up and give up more! It is one more 'guilt inducer' as people don't want to give things up. Little is offered to replace those things. Religion is sterile, cold, even boring. But the truth is, when love is present and strong and the foremost emotion, then giving up for the lover's sake is no hardship. The lover, his desires, that which pleases him, is all important; all else is perceived as inferior. When the believer is so overwhelmed with the love of God, then the giving up of things is a delight of love rather than a hardship.

When Andy was first saved, in the throes of first love, when Jesus was all, God graciously pointed to that which had been a long time love affair. It was a romance with music, particularly 'Tamla Motown', soul music. Over the years Andy had built up a prized collection of original singles, many imported from the States. In those early days of love for Jesus, all other loves became as nothing. When God pointed to the idolatry of this other love, parting with the record collection was not a hardship – it was a delight! 'God, thank you for a stripping away of other loves that love may be single, concentrated, deeper.' Of course, in the intervening years other loves have again encroached on that one true love and there have been many dealings with God, many returns to the first love of Jesus. Whenever mere religious duty was present, what God demanded was hard and reluctantly given. Whenever his love was strong, that which he required became an easy yoke, a light burden, a loving response to his love poured into the heart.

There is even a deeper sense still in which longing for God is to be weaned from our old self with its inner corruption and opposition to Christ. It is the deep desire to be led away by Christ from the inner drives which dominate us so often. The clearest biblical example of this is Paul in Romans 7:24. Having described his own struggle with sin and its pulling him down he utters these words: 'Wretched man that I am! Who will rescue me from this body of death?' That is the deep inner spiritual longing of the apostle, to be drawn after Christ.

Some have said, 'Surely, this cannot be the cry of a spiritual person who should rather be victorious in God.' In truth, this is the cry of the most spiritual believer in Christ. It is the desire to be led away from the flesh and led into a deeper relationship with Christ. We know that even in those who are mature the flesh rears itself in pride, in boasting, in unbelief and disobedience. Those who love Christ the most love the flesh the least and cry from the depth of their being, 'Lord lead me away . . . draw me away. Lord I will gladly run after you.'

Beware the flattery of Solomon!

Another lesson of love from this first chapter is found in the latter part of verse 4. Even though the king had brought her into his chambers, 'we will exult and rejoice in you'. For this young girl, being separated from the shepherd in the court of Solomon only causes her to remember the shepherd.

If the enemy cannot get you by attacking you, he will flatter you, he will give you riches and responsibilities. During the Song, a number of times Solomon seeks to win the girl's love by flattery. We have seen numbers of people who start well in Christ but who are led down this path. It is often the younger folk, converted in their teens and on fire for God. After walking with him for some time they go off to university, keen to serve, and join in the Christian Union. But then comes the job, the family and all the responsibilities associated with growing maturity. Job promotion, nice house, better car – Solomon flatters. It is the king's chambers for them, so to speak, and they lose their first love.

But not the Shulammite in the Song. Faced with all Solomon's wealth she remembers her beloved. May it be so for us. Join the Shulammite in your prayer to God:

Let him kiss me . . . Lord, may I know the direct, personal expression of your love for me. Lord, reveal your love, manifest your love in my heart and soul.

CHAPTER 2

THE BELOVED'S SELF-REVELATION

I am black and beautiful,
O daughters of Jerusalem,
like the tents of Kedar,
like the curtains of Solomon.
Do not gaze at me because I am dark,
because the sun has gazed on me.
My mother's sons were angry with me;
they made me keeper of the vineyards,
but my own vineyard I have not kept!

Song 1:5–6

Shepherding has always been a noble profession. In the Israel of Solomon's day, shepherding was a demanding task requiring great personal commitment to a life lived in the open air. It required personal courage and fortitude, as long and dangerous journeys were often required. Life in the wilds was not the best thing for your complexion! In the Song we find a young shepherdess, taken from her familiar outdoor surroundings and given a place among the women of Jerusalem, the harem of king Solomon. She is, however, lovesick for her beloved shepherd, and in her longing for her lover she reflects on her own life.

The other women in the harem look down on the newcomer. They stare at her. She is not as refined as many of them. They marvel that Solomon could think so highly of this rustic girl. What does he see in her? Their jealousy is obvious. Her sun-darkened skin becomes a point of ridicule.

She defends herself in the words, 'I am black and beautiful, O daughters of Jerusalem.' It is not her fault that she has spent so much time under the scorching sun. To this point life has not been kind to this young girl. Even her own brothers have been angry with her. The Shulammite does not reveal why, but tells us that their anger led them to give her extra work to the neglect of herself. She compares herself to a vineyard which she has neglected to look after other vineyards. She has cared for others at the expense of herself.

Over the years we have cared for many foster children. Karen came to us when she had just turned thirteen. Like a number of girls we have cared for, Karen, in the force of circumstances, had been made to care for 'other vineyards' to the neglect of her own. From very young she had missed out on the things of childhood and taken on the parenting task for her younger brothers and sisters. Indeed, she had taken on the immense task of mothering and caring for her own alcoholic mother. She ensured the other children got up in time for school. She made their breakfasts. After school, in the evening, Karen opened the tin of baked beans and tried to keep the little ones nourished. When mother was in a drunken state it was Karen who protected her brothers and sisters from the worst excesses of violence.

One of our primary tasks with Karen was to allow her opportunity to 'keep her own vineyard', to care for herself in a way that had never happened to that date. There were affirming experiences that she had missed in early childhood which we helped her to find.

Karen reminded us of the Shulammite. Thankfully, the girl in the Song was aware of her situation. Later in the story the shepherd, through his love and affirmation of her beauty, restores the girl. She becomes for him, not a neglected vineyard, but a beautiful garden (4:12). She in turn responds to her lover with an acknowledgment of her own beauty (4:16).

But at this time it is no wonder that she did not match up in the eyes of the other court women. She was somewhat unrefined. There had been self-neglect. And yet there was about her a raw natural beauty that none of the court women could match. It was that which had drawn Solomon to her when he saw her for the first time in the garden of nuts. In fact, she realised herself that there was in her something of beauty; 'I am black and beautiful'.

Self-understanding

The scene is rich in allegory and revelation of God's ways with us. Of significance is the self-revelation which the girl finds arising from her own heart longing, and from the things she suffers at the hands of others. It is contained in the phrase 'black and beautiful'.

Paul gave this counsel to the Romans:

> For by the grace given to me I say to everyone among you not to think of yourself more highly than you ought to think, but to think with sober judgment, each according to the measure of faith that God has assigned.
>
> Romans 12:3

There is a need for every one of us to see ourselves in the way God sees us. There must be something of sobriety in the way we perceive ourselves. As in most things there are extremes to be avoided. Our society is, in many ways, dominated by a 'cult of the self'. We are encouraged to find self-worth, to be self-assertive and to love ourselves. Our culture is dominated by what philosophers have called 'emotivism'. Each does that which they 'feel' is right for them. Self has been enthroned as king and is always right. It is a far cry from the self-revelation which comes to us before God. In God's presence we reckon with the reality of sin; not merely the things we do wrong, but the very essence of a heart in its natural state opposed to God and his goodness. In the presence of a holy God sin is always exposed. Self-knowledge which has no room for sin is false knowledge.

But there is another extreme. It is the extreme of the 'miserable worm'. There have been Christian theologies, and many of us carry these around in our hearts, which see nothing good in us at all. It is a negation of the self, seeing ourselves as utterly worthless. It is an extreme which captures many of God's dearest friends and weights them down with an intolerable burden. It is an incapacitating error which stifles the work of God and quenches the Spirit. The truth is that God looks upon us with immense longing in his heart and sees in us something of intense beauty.

The Shulammite's self-revelation was balanced. She recognised that she was both black, scorched by the heat of the sun *and* beautiful to her beloved shepherd. In our allegorising she knew both the depths of remaining sin *and* her worth to the Saviour. She lived in the paradox of those extremes. Both were truth and neither was truth in isolation.

In the recent times of refreshing we have experienced the amazing, overwhelming revelation of the Father's love. We can honestly say that we have never known such intensity, such intimacy. God's revelation has caused us to laugh and to cry, to lose bodily strength and yet to be filled with energy! There has also been self-revelation which has been a painful experience.

One evening, all hell seemed to be loosed upon us. One of our children was involved in a situation at school which was blown out of all proportion. It should have been a situation easily defused with wrongs righted in simple Christian love. But family life is often not simple. There are all kinds of conflicting expectations, hopes, fears and insecurities. On this occasion they all seemed to surface with the force of a Trident nuclear submarine! The worst of it was not the situation itself, but our reaction to unforeseen circumstances. Tempers were lost, unkind words spoken and many tears shed. God, who had been opening to us such a revelation of his love and acceptance, gave us a sight of our remaining inner sinfulness. It is not an over-exaggeration to say that we were devastated! The sight of self, of inner corruption, having seen so much of God, was almost unbearable. We remained in that awful place of knowing the magnificence of

God and the abject poverty of ourselves for some forty-eight-hours. It was one of the most painful experiences we have ever passed through.

Job, Isaiah and John

It has always been that way. God's saints from Job, to Isaiah, to John in the Revelation have found it to be so.

Job passed through a great deal; probably more than any of us, certainly more than we have passed through. It is not a criticism to say that Job did not always bear his trials in the best way. Much of it he did, probably better than we would. But it was not until God revealed his glory to Job in the last few chapters of the book that Job really saw himself before God's holiness. Having soaked in the presence of God, his conclusion was quite simple:

> I had heard of you by the hearing of the ear, but now my eye sees you; therefore I despise myself, and repent in dust and ashes.
>
> Job 42:5–6

Heart revelation of God led Job to an inner revelation of himself. Isaiah and John were led along the same route. Isaiah saw God high and lifted up. His glory was dazzling! Amazing! Yet it exposed the inner corruption of his heart. He felt unclean, poor, pitiful and unworthy.

> And I said: 'Woe is me! I am lost, for I am a man of unclean lips, and I live among a people of unclean lips. . .yet my eyes have seen the King, the LORD of hosts!'
>
> Isaiah 6:5

God gave to John a wonderful revelation. It stands as one of the most beautiful and awesome descriptions of the risen and ascended Jesus.

> Then I turned to see whose voice it was that spoke to me, and on turning I saw seven golden lampstands, and in the midst of the lampstands I saw one like the Son of Man, clothed with a long robe and with a golden sash across his chest. His head and his hair were

white as white wool, white as snow; his eyes were like a flame of fire, his feet were like burnished bronze, refined as in a furnace, and his voice was like the sound of many waters. In his right hand he held seven stars, and from his mouth came a sharp, two-edged sword, and his face was like the sun shining with full force.

Revelation 1:12–16

John's response was immediate and clear: 'When I saw him, I fell at his feet as though dead' (v17). The sight of Jesus caused such a self-revelation for John, that his only response was to fall before God as one who was dead.

But the exposure of inner corruption is never an end in itself. Job was blessed more in the latter part of his life than in the early parts. Isaiah was used by God as one of the greatest prophets and given the clearest prophecies in all Scripture of the coming Messiah. John, after his self-revelation and cleansing, was the recipient of the great revelation of the Lamb's triumph over Satan.

Were God merely to reveal the inner corruption of our hearts and leave us, it would make him a capricious, even a cruel, deity. Allowing us to see ourselves is only ever to open the way for cleansing, transformation and further blessing as God pours yet more of his love into our lives.

Our forty-eight hours of the agony of self-knowledge in the light of God's purity and goodness led to a further experience of deep cleansing and the release of forgiveness. Jane, worshipping in God's presence, interacting with the work of the Spirit, felt God speak: 'I have allowed you to taste death. You will now experience the resurrection.' Over the next two days we both experienced the most powerful touch of God, with such an increase of depth – more than we could have imagined.' He communicated again to us how much we are to him.

Black and beautiful

The self-revelation of inner corruption is only half the story and not the most enduring part of the story. The simple and beautiful truth is that God has always loved us. He loved us when we were his enemies. He loved us when we sinned our very worst. There is no great achievement we could do to make him love us more, and there is no heinous sin we could commit to make him love us less. God loves us. He wants to communicate that love deep in our spirits; to saturate our hearts with it; to renew our minds with all the creative potential that such an astonishing fact releases.

Our suspicion is that for most of us seeing our own inner corruption is the easier revelation. We can believe that God is good and loving. We know all too well that we are often far less than we would want ourselves, let alone God, to be. But the thought that God sees in us something of beauty is beyond our belief.

Andy was with a good friend who had fallen hopelessly in love with a girl. He was eager to meet her and asked innocently for a description, so that he would have a picture in his mind of the young woman he was to look out for. The good friend began to describe her – the colour of her eyes, the style of her hair, the shape of her nose, the dimples in her cheeks. He concluded: 'Andy, you will agree with me that she is the most beautiful person in the world.' Andy couldn't wait! As it turned out, she was indeed a pretty girl, and the friend's description was true – up to a point. But his was the language of love flowing from the deepest of human emotions. He perceived in her a beauty which equated somewhat to her natural appearance, but his comments also spoke eloquently of *his* love for her. He found her to be beautiful irrespective of Andy's feelings on the matter, or anybody else's as it happens!

That is the way Jesus sees each of us. To him we are beautiful, and his desire is to communicate to our hearts how much beauty he sees in us.

To receive that, for those of us schooled in evangelical teaching, is hard. We have so emphasised our sin, God's judgement, and the need for salvation, that in our consciousness the most prominent self-understanding is of being sinners. It is hard for us to hold the paradox of our inner corruption and rebellion and our created beauty which God looks upon restored through Jesus. The truth in our minds 'God loves you' needs to envelop and saturate our spirits. We need an inner revelation which comes through spending much time in the presence of God.

Thankfully, the girl in the Song realised the truth that to her lover she was beautiful.

Taking care of the vineyards

There is a further aspect to her self-understanding. The Shulammite realises that she has cared for others to the neglect of herself. Caring for others is a primary Christian responsibility. We all learned the little dictum, 'God first, others second, self last'. Like many simple sayings there is truth, but not the whole truth. In terms of our spiritual life and development we will only be of use to others if we are first in a good relationship with God ourselves. We can only bring others as far as we have gone ourselves.

In spiritual terms many churches are poverty stricken. No doubt there are a few bright lights of spirituality in most congregations. In general, our experience is that most Christians know God only a little. Of course, many know doctrines. Many Christians can spot a heresy from a great distance! But in terms of a deep relationship of love with Father, Son and Holy Spirit many of us have not reached first base. We have substituted head knowledge and activity for the deeper things of God, and those of us in leadership must take at least part of the responsibility.

Some years ago God spoke very clearly to Andy in these words 'Many a minister has buried their spirituality in the grave of their activities.' It was a powerful word and yet one neglected through many excuses. 'I realise that, Lord, but I have such and such to prepare, so and so to see, so much administration to do . . . When I have finished all that I will consider what you are saying.' For many of God's leaders the girl's words are all too true: 'They made me keeper of the vineyards, but my own vineyard I have not kept.' How can we lead others to God when we scarcely know him ourselves? How can we fan the flames of love for Jesus in the people we shepherd when the flame is all but quenched in our own lives?

There is a need of radical change. The extraneous and unnecessary baggage we have accumulated over the years needs to be urgently jettisoned. We need to throw out the agenda forced upon us by others' expectations and learn to live according to God's agenda. At the top of which is to know Father more deeply, to fall in love with Jesus, and to be daily saturated in the Holy Spirit. We are convinced that if we care for our own vineyards in this way, others will be helped in the best way.

Where the shepherd feeds his flock

> Tell me, you whom my soul loves, where you pasture your flock, where you make it lie down at noon; for why should I be like one who is veiled beside the flocks of your companions?
> If you do not know, O fairest among women, follow the tracks of the flock, and pasture your kids beside the shepherds' tents.
>
> Song 1:7–8

Receiving malicious criticism is never easy. For this young girl it causes her heart to long all the more for her shepherd lover. Her inner being cries out for the shepherd to tell her where he is. The answer comes, surprisingly, from the other women who seem to take pity upon her and give her advice. They even call her the 'fairest among women'. Their earlier mocking is turned to kindness. Perhaps they realised how deeply alone she felt. The counsel of the women is quite simple: to find the shepherd, find the flock which he is caring for.

There is, here, an important principle. We need to be in the place where the shepherd is feeding the flock. Many of God's people find themselves in places spiritually separated from the shepherd. Faithfully, week by week they attend

Christian services which are spiritually dry and where there is little satisfying pasture. They continue year after year in the belief that one day God will bring renewal. Sometimes he does and we are grateful. But time is short. We each have only a short time, and our priority is to find where our shepherd is.

Money can't buy me love

> I compare you, my love,
> to a mare among Pharaoh's chariots.
> Your cheeks are comely with ornaments,
> your neck with strings of jewels.
> We will make you ornaments of gold,
> studded with silver.

Song 1:9–11

This opening scene in the song ends with the words of Solomon. He expresses his appreciation of the girl and gives her the promise of riches and wealth 'ornaments of gold, studded with silver'. In many interpretations of the Song, these words are taken as words of love. In the outline we are following we take them as words of flattery wedded to incentives to stay away from the shepherd lover.

There have always been those who have believed that love can be bought. Wisdom comes from the unlikeliest of sources. Even the early Beatles realised that 'money can't buy me love'! Solomon, full of God-given wisdom, had not, as yet, realised that truth.

Solomon's speech concludes the first part of the Song. It is a scene of separation which gives us insight into the heart longing of the girl, the ridicule and mocking which she suffers from others and the king's flattery and attempt to win her through his riches.

CHAPTER 3

'WORDS OF LOVE YOU WHISPER SOFT AND TRUE ...'
(Buddy Holly)

The Song of Songs allows us the privileged glimpse of the intimacy of love between two young lovers. In the normal course of events we are not a party to the 'whispering of sweet nothings' which, thankfully, happen for all who fall in love. The Song, however, gives us an insider's view.

Grown women and men find themselves saying, in the intimacy of the lover's embrace, things which would normally not enter their heads. Sentiments expressing the inner longings, desires and feelings often tumble out, one on top of another.

It is something akin to that which happens to parents as they pour love upon their new born baby. 'You're a beautiful little fellow ... ' (strange gurgling noises made by loving parent as she blows a raspberry on baby's tummy), 'yes you are, yes you are' (repeated any number of times) ... 'and mummy loves you ... yes she does ... ' more strange behaviour ... etc. Parental love melts the hardest of hearts. Sane, rational people engage in the strangest of behaviour as they pour love upon a baby human being who doesn't understand the talk anyway!

Words of love between those deeply in love bear many resemblances. If we were to examine them in the 'cold light of day', the chances are that we would be somewhat embarrassed. 'I said that ... !' There is sound advice in the book on marriage which urges that intimate words spoken in the fullness of love are not to be openly repeated to others. Such words spring from the inner being, from the heart. The writer to the Hebrews urges us: 'Let marriage be held in honour by all, and let the marriage bed be kept undefiled . . .' (Heb 13:4a). The primary reference is, of course, to those who would violate marriage through adultery. But there is something of holiness about deep, loving relationships. There is something deeply personal and intense, and into which we are not to invite others.

Yet God in his wisdom has allowed us a glimpse into such a relationship in the Song. We are the privileged 'guests' during intimate moments of love between the shepherd and shepherdess.

Courtship love

While the king was on his couch,
my nard gave forth its fragrance.

Song 1:12

In this second section of the Song we find the two young lovers together for the first time in the poem. Though they had been forcibly separated, for a brief while they are back together again. It seems that while king Solomon was on his couch, possibly resting after a meal, the shepherdess finds an opportunity to renew her love with the beloved shepherd. She leaves Solomon and the young lovers snatch an embrace in which they renew words of love for one another.

In the interpretation we are following this is the first of three periods together. It is a period of courtship. In this section there is the fervency of love, but love which is not yet consummated in marriage. The lovers know one another, but there is not yet the depth of intimacy which we find later in the Song.

This period is followed by another one of separation in which love is tested, followed by a growing deepening of love in more intimate descriptions of their life together.

Some commentators recognise chapters four and five as the wedding night of the two lovers. We will follow this interpretation as there is very clearly a much deeper love than we find in chapter two. The descriptions of intimacy are greater and the lovers' appreciation of one another is all the more intense. Yet even consummated love is tested, perhaps more severely than previous testings. The final period together, which does not end, is found in chapters six to eight and is the fullness of mature love.

For now, we are concerned with the fervent love of courtship. Love is new, desperate and intense. It is the period of love where thoughts are constantly filled with images of the lover. It is where a day without the lover passes infinitely slowly and when time in the lover's arms passes all too quickly. The inner longing is to be together and to remain together, never having to part.

It was Christmas Eve 1974. We had been courting for only a few short weeks, but love was intense. Jane drove Andy home from work to his parents' house and was preparing to drive over to her parents for Christmas. The forty-four miles seemed like the other end of the world. Andy hovered at the doorway as Jane played with her car keys. Neither wanted the brief meeting together to end. They would be parted for three days . . . it felt like it would be forever. In the end Jane forced herself to get into the car and drive away. Andy watched her until the car turned a corner. She was gone. Within two hours the phone rang at the Fitz-Gibbon home. 'I made it. I'm missing you already . . . ' Christmas 1974 had an amazingly bitter-sweet quality to it. There was the sheer excitement of courtship love and the pain of parting. We knew instinctively and deeply that we were to be together.

The feeling is as old as humanity. It is part of the Creator's order. However much we are told that marriage is an outdated concept, and however far we move as a society towards serial relationships, there is still this inner constraint of love to find one to be together with. And not merely for a brief period, not merely for self-gratification, but something of the permanency of human togetherness which all but defies description. It is here that we find the lovers in the Song.

My beloved is to me a bag of myrrh
that lies between my breasts.
My beloved is to me a cluster of henna blossoms
in the vineyards of En-gedi.

Ah, you are beautiful, my love;
ah, you are beautiful;
your eyes are doves.

Ah, you are beautiful, my beloved, truly lovely.
Our couch is green;
the beams of our house are cedar,
our rafters are pine.
I am a rose of Sharon,
a lily of the valleys.

As a lily among brambles,
so is my love among maidens.

As an apple tree among the trees of the wood,
so is my beloved among young men.
With great delight I sat in his shadow,
and his fruit was sweet to my taste.
He brought me to the banqueting house,
and his intention toward me was love.
Sustain me with raisins,
refresh me with apples;
for I am faint with love.
O that his left hand were under my head,
and that his right hand embraced me!
I adjure you, O daughters of Jerusalem,
by the gazelles or the wild does:
do not stir up or awaken love until it is ready!

Song 1:13–2:7

At this point in their relationship, expressions of their love are given mostly by the young girl. In their renewed togetherness she pours our her heart to the shepherd. His response is more measured, yet nonetheless intense in his affirmation of her beauty.

Her longings of the first part of the Song are realised as she finds herself in her beloved's arms. It has for her that almost unbelievable quality. He is here at last! And his intentions are only of love towards her! She is 'faint with love'. Lovesick! And yet there is clearly not the consummation which they both long for. She desires with her whole being that time when 'his left hand were under my head, and that his right hand [would] embrace me!'

Sick with love!

It points us to an essential time in spiritual life when, like the shepherdess, we are 'faint with love' for our Saviour Jesus. It is not the deepest point of relationship with God, but an essential aspect in its development towards maturity. Simply put, there needs to be a time when we are consumed with courtship passion for Jesus.

Religion is often sterile and cold. Christianity is, in many respects, unattractive to unbelievers today. There is little fire. It presents itself mostly as a philosophy to the mind. Christianity is, a reasonable belief system alongside other world views. When people make commitments to Christ in this framework, the resulting Christian life is mostly centred around understanding Christian teaching and striving to apply it.

But the very heart of Christianity is about relationship with the risen Lord who is not a doctrine or a philosophy, but a person who desires more than anything to enter into loving communion with the people he created.

Our fourteen year old son was sharing with us the difficulty he had experienced in telling his friends about Jesus. He said, 'Mum, I tried to get the point across to them that it was not the Christian religion but the Christian relationship which counts.' Ben had latched onto something of immense importance. The Christian religion will not make a difference in our world. The Christian relationship will.

The book of Acts is the story of how ordinary people entered into the Christian relationship and turned the world upside down.

> Now when they saw the boldness of Peter and John and realised that they were uneducated and ordinary men, they were amazed and recognised them as companions of Jesus.
>
> Acts 4:13

The King James Version says, 'they took knowledge of them, that *they had been with Jesus*.' Christianity as mere religion is not life transforming. Christianity as being with Jesus transforms us, and through us turns the world upside down.

Fervent Christianity, full of fire, horrifies most of us! It has always been offensive to the natural person. In days of revival it was disparagingly termed 'enthusiasm'. Those with enthusiasm could be easily dismissed as those on the fringe. The mainstream of the church would continue in its established, thoughtful ways. And the world would remain unchanged!

But the truth is, the Christian church has had the most effect on the world when Christians have entered into a deep, loving relationship with Christ which fires their hearts and which outwardly looks suspiciously like enthusiasm at best, and fanaticism at worst!

The desperate need of all Christians is to know courtship-love with Jesus which saturates heart and mind and which throws every other consideration into the shadows. It is not, firstly, trying to work ourselves up into it. It will not arise out of striving to love him more. It comes through his revelation to our hearts that we are loved by him.

> Ah, you are beautiful, my love;
> ah, you are beautiful;
> your eyes are doves.
>
> Song 1:15

These words spoken by the shepherd to his lover are words which the Lord Jesus Christ reveals to our hearts. In each of us there is a beauty which Christ affirms as he speaks words of love to our spirits. He repeats himself to convince us of his love. 'You are beautiful' . . . 'Surely, Lord, you can't mean me?' . . . 'Yes, you . . . even *you* . . . are beautiful. There is something about you of the dove, of the Spirit. I see such beauty in you.'

Such outpourings of love elicit love in response. When he once speaks deeply into us and we receive the revelation of his love then we can only respond with fervent love ourselves. His love draws our love towards him. It can only be that way. Even at its best our love is always reflection, always response.

The words the Shulammite utters to the shepherd are deeply personal. They speak to us of intimate dialogue in the Spirit between us and God. We need to move beyond the mere formality of prayers and into the openness of the language of love.

In marriage preparation classes, one of the things we tell engaged couples is that the positive and frequent expressions of love for one another are of the utmost importance. We ask, 'Sue, has Tom told you often how much he loves you?' 'Have you told him today that you love him?' We are delighted when we are met with blushing cheeks, a coy look, a grasping of the lover's hand and words to the effect that 'Of course, we love each other deeply!' We are more worried when we are faced with a couple who feel such expressions of love to be mere banalities: 'Our relationship is not that kind, thank your very much!'

In our experience, if there is not the fervency of love and loving expression in the courtship stage, then marriage is going to prove very hard indeed.

Springing from his heart of love God desires our love in return. 'God, I think very highly of you, but don't want to get into this love stuff' will not do it. Christianity which is merely concerned with the formulations of right doctrine, or with speculating on the nature of the Trinity, or with trying to organise the best church, is a long way from God's heart.

The fervency of courtship-love is essential. In the spiritual life it cannot be bypassed. It is a basic building block of deeper relationship with God providing a foundation for all that follows.

It can be seen as selfish love. There is so much happening in the world and all you care about, can even think about, is your love relationship with Jesus. Finding young Christians with their 'heads in the clouds' can be frustrating to older believers. Even worse, in their enthusiasm they make all kinds of mistakes, say all kinds of silly things and profess the most heinous heresies! Who cares! Fiery courtship-love turns the world upside down. Oh, that there were more and more such fervent believers!

Some of us may need to return to this stage of our relationship with God. It's quite possible that we became Christians in a dry period where we had no model of fervency. In the recent times of refreshing God is revealing again his passionate love for us. The direction of our hearts is towards fervency. Many of us who have been Christians for years will find ourselves, quite possibly for the first time, overwhelmed with courtship-love for God. Like the shepherdess we will become 'faint with love' as we receive in our spirits God's loving communication.

'God, please reveal your love in ever greater measure to my heart. May I know the fervency of courtship-love. Fill my mind, feelings, entire being with an overwhelming sense of your love. Help me to express my love to you from the depth of my heart.'

CHAPTER 4

THE BELOVED'S INNER LIFE

Do not adorn yourselves outwardly by braiding your hair, and by wearing gold ornaments or fine clothing; rather, *let your adornment be the inner self with the lasting beauty of a gentle and quiet spirit, which is very precious in God's sight.* (Our italics)

1 Peter 3:3–4

But the LORD said to Samuel, 'Do not look on his appearance or on the height of his stature, because I have rejected him; for the LORD does not see as mortals see; *they look on the outward appearance, but the LORD looks on the heart.*' (Our italics)

1 Samuel 16:7

We want to spend a little more time with the period of togetherness in chapters 1 and 2. Partly because of the immense importance of this period in their relationship, and partly because it will help us grasp principles of interpretation, both for this and other parts of the Song.

To interpret the poem there is need both to understand the language of metaphor and the application of allegory. Before we try to make an application of the Song to our life with God, it is important to realise that many of the descriptions within it are figures of speech. If we can understand these metaphors, then we will be able to make a more satisfactory application of them.

Our daughter Rebekah has always enjoyed dressing up in 'play clothes' and making herself pretty. Often we would say to her 'Oh, you look just like a princess!' Of course, we were using language figuratively to express how beautiful she looked to us. Similarly, if you have a friend who is somewhat down you might say, 'What's the matter with you? You've got a face like a fiddle!' Not the most flattering thing to say, but very descriptive of a long 'hang-dog' expression . . . but there we go again, using figurative language! Metaphor is very important in everyday speech. Actually, it's quite difficult to describe things without using figures of speech.

It's also quite clear, then, that a deep relationship of love is exceedingly difficult to put into words. Both lovers in the Song, therefore, resort to more oblique language to try to describe the depths of their inner feelings. In the nature of things (because both partners are familiar with the pastoral life) many of their figures of speech relate to the life of the country. In this first encounter, then, we need to realise that though there is talk of 'doves, raisins and apples', it is not a poem about the pleasures of the countryside! Each of these descriptions is a figurative and beautiful way to describe aspects of their love, their intimacy and their desire.

In Chapter 1 verses 12–14 the Shulammite three times speaks of perfume or fragrance: nard, a bag of myrrh and a cluster of henna blossoms. In verse 12 the sense is this: 'While Solomon is reclining on his couch my beloved shepherd is to me as nard (a beautiful aromatic gum). There is that of the fragrance of love about my beloved. He has the scent of love about him which draws me towards him like the finest of perfume.' She continues with these musings about love with the deeper thought that, even while she sleeps, it is as if her beloved shepherd is like a bag of myrrh close to her heart. Her every thought at night is of him. His scent is with her all the time. The feeling is so overwhelming that she expresses it in a third way, 'a cluster of henna blossoms'. There is an extravagance about her love for the shepherd! Her loving descriptions tumble one on top of another.

The shepherd's response is more measured and he focuses his words on her eyes.[1] She has captivated him. He sees such beauty in her eyes that on the three occasions in which we find them together he mentions them. In chapter 4 her eyes are the very first aspect of her beauty which he mentions, again using the figure of doves to describe them. There is a clarity, a softness and a purity about her eyes which staggers him.

It has rightly been said that the eyes are a window to the soul. That's why it is difficult to tell lies and look someone directly in the eyes. It's also why, if you have a difficulty with someone, it is hard to look at them confidently. When a mother looks at her new born child there is what amounts to a deep and intimate look of recognition as their eyes meet.

More to the point, for our purposes, when lovers gaze into each other's eyes they look deeply into the other's heart. In the Song, the shepherd is so overwhelmed by the look in her eyes, in their third encounter together (when love is at its most mature), the shepherd even urges his wife to 'Turn away your eyes from me, for they overwhelm me!'

In this first loving encounter, the metaphor of 'dove's eyes' seems to suggest that he is admiring the utter sincerity, purity and love which he finds as he looks into the eyes of his bride to be.

She responds, mirroring his affirmation of beauty, and further describes their love in terms of the wild beauty of the forest. Theirs is a love of the open air, a natural, unforced love.

But at this point she still has a natural reticence about his overwhelming affirmation of her. Chapter 2 begins with the sense 'but I am only a rose of Sharon, a lily of the valleys. I am merely a wild flower, the kind of which there is a profusion. How can you say so much about me? How can you see such beauty in me?'

The shepherd replies with the astonishing thought, to her, that all others are to him like brambles, while she is a delicate and beautiful lily.

As if the penny drops and she truly realises his love for her, she begins to pour out her love and longing for more of the shepherd. Compared to other young men who are merely trees of the wood, the shepherd is an apple tree. There is about him that which deeply satisfies her. And if he is as an apple tree, then she would sit in his shade, sheltering her from the blazing sun which has scorched her.

As an apple tree her beloved would feed her with delightful fruit. Of course she is not speaking of eating literal apples. She is speaking of the delight she has found in the love of the shepherd. His love is that which feeds her as the choicest fruit; sweet, appetising, delicious. And it is not merely fantasy. She has tasted and found the fruit of his love to be truly satisfying.

The remaining part of her speech (2:4–7) is again figurative and points to her enjoyment of their relationship. The banqueting house is the place of love, not a literal place, but that arena between two souls who have become intertwined at a deep level. It is that place where they enjoy one another in the fullest way. She admits that love between them is so strong that she is lovesick and needs to be sustained. Yet the paradox of love is that lovesickness is sustained by more love! Raisins and apples are again figures of speech to describe the shepherd's satisfying love of the Shulammite.

In case we had missed the point, the young girl becomes more explicit in her speech. She moves away from metaphor and speaks plainly of her longing: 'O that his left hand were under my head, and that his right hand embraced me!' It is a longing which she remembers later in chapter 8:3 and is the desire of lovers for the greatest of intimacy. In both instances the longing is followed by the general urging to allow love to follow its own course and not to disturb it until it is ready. There is for her at this point a deep desire to rest in the love of the shepherd and not to be disturbed by others.

The priority of the inner life

To this point we have merely tried to 'unpack' the use of metaphor in the poem, to uncover the best 'plain' meaning before we attempt to find an allegorical interpretation. If we are correct, then the spiritual meaning is clear, and you will have been making your own application as you have read so far. The passage speaks to us of the depth of the believer's inner life; our inner life of loving relationship with God.

There is a remarkable contrast in this emphasis on the inner relationship with that in chapter 1:9–11 where Solomon recognises the natural and raw beauty of the young girl as 'a mare among Pharaoh's chariots'. Solomon, however, wants to cover this raw and natural beauty with 'ornaments of gold, studded with silver.' In other words, his love for her remains at the outward level. Between the shepherd and the Shulammite there is the depth of intimacy of the inner relationship. Solomon, who did not have that depth of relationship (he did not have her heart, for she belonged to another), wanted the relationship to be merely outward.

This speaks to us very much of the important biblical principle of the inner and the outer. Very clearly, to God the most important aspect of our lives is that which is on the inside. It is not what people see, but what God sees which counts. So often we look on the outer appearance; God looks on the heart. This principle was stated clearly to Samuel in the choice of a king. It was reiterated by Peter to the godly women of the church. We dress up to put on an appearance of beauty; God urges us to be adorned internally with beauty, in fact with his beauty. Paul keyed into this idea a number of times: 'So we do not lose heart. Even though our outer nature is wasting away, our inner nature is being renewed day by day' (2 Cor 4:16). 'I pray that, according to the riches of his glory, he may grant that you may be strengthened in your inner being with power through his spirit' (Eph 3:16).

It is a lesson we need to learn and learn again. There is with all of us a propensity to neglect the inner and to concentrate on the outer. Solomon stands for anything which would rival the Lord Jesus Christ in our affections, and which would distract us from the inner consciousness of intimacy with him.

Christianity has become for many of us an exercise in the externals of religion. There are many good ways in which we might adorn ourselves with the outward and ignore that which is most important, the inner relationship with him. If fact, most of us have become quite successful at it. Even Christian things, which are often good and necessary for Christian growth, can take us from this inner relationship.

We want to list some of these, not in any sense to bring others into condemnation, but to identify ways in which we have substituted the outward for the inner.

Perhaps the easiest to fall into is Christian service. We know and love the Lord and desire to serve him. We offer ourselves for service, receive training and find ourselves in a position of responsibility in some part of God's work. But gradually and imperceptibly (if it was sudden and obvious we would be more guarded) the work of God becomes a substitute for God himself. The truth is that many pastors carry out the profession of ministry years after having lost their courtship-love relationship with Jesus. Many church members go through the religious motions of church week after week with hearts unmoved by the love of the shepherd at any deep level. A number of scriptures speak to us with this regard.

> Now while Jesus was at Bethany in the house of Simon the leper, a woman came to him with an alabaster jar of very costly ointment, and she poured it on his head as he sat at the table. But when the disciples saw it, they were angry and said, 'Why this waste? For this ointment could have been sold for a large sum, and the money given to the poor.'
>
> Mt 26:6–9

> Now as they went on their way, he entered a certain village, where a woman named Martha welcomed him into her home. She had a sister named Mary, who sat at the Lord's feet and listened to what he was saying. But Martha was distracted by her many tasks; so she came to him and asked, 'Lord, do you not care that my sister has left me to do all the work by myself? Tell her then to help me.' But the Lord answered her, 'Martha, Martha, you are worried and distracted

by many things; there is need of only one thing. Mary has chosen the better part, which will not be taken away from her.'

Lk 10:38–42

Both women had learnt to 'waste' themselves on Jesus alone, to pour out themselves in relationship with him.

It might be that some of us need purposely to lay down ministries and service which have become merely a work of the flesh without the heartbeat of love for Jesus. 'But I love the work I do. It's important. People rely on me.' That may reach to the core of the problem. We love the work of God rather than God himself. We have led people into a dependency on *us* rather than into a love relationship with *him*. In the times of refreshing, God is bringing us back to intimacy with him. Many pastors have testified that God's work had become something of a substitute for the deeper knowledge of God.

There is another area which may prove difficult for evangelical Bible believers. Many of us love the book and have missed the author! The warning was given very clearly by Jesus in these words: 'You search the scriptures because you think that in them you have eternal life; and it is they that testify on my behalf. *Yet you refuse to come to me to have life* (John 5:39–40, our italics). Still we have not listened. We have so elevated the Scriptures that it is a brave soul who suggests that we have made the Bible into an idol. Yet we have done so!

Rightly we have emphasised the teaching that Christianity is a revealed religion and that the only way we can know God is through his self-revelation. That self-revelation is supremely in the Bible, therefore, we need to know the Bible. But the Bible is not an end in itself, and we have more often than not made it an end. Thousands upon thousands of sermons are preached week after week, thousands of books about the Bible pour off the Christian presses with amazing regularity; thousands of tapes and videos are made, listened to and watched . . . but to what end? We have 'never had it so good' in our understanding and helps in Bible study. However, if any and all of that does not lead us into intimacy with God, then it is futile and a waste of time and energy. Perhaps even worse, it becomes a deception. We know the Bible so we think we know the Lord. It was not the case when our Saviour spoke to the Pharisees, and it is not the case now.

The story of Mary and Martha and the anointing of Jesus has even been used to suggest that Christians ought, like Mary, to be involved in more Bible study. Mary's simply sitting at the feet of Jesus is equated with reading about Jesus in the Scriptures. This view is hardly ever challenged in evangelical circles. More Bible knowledge is not more of Jesus. He is present now through the Spirit and being with Jesus, knowing him ever deeper, is a matter of spiritual reality, not merely Bible study.

In the last thirty years there has been a revolution in the way the church worships. Archaic language has been replaced by current idiom. In God's goodness thousands of new songs have been written. Musical styles have developed and have become more culturally relevant to the newer generations. Worship has become for many of us a good experience, no longer stuffy, no longer boring. But again, if worship becomes merely outward, merely a form, and does not lead us to intimacy with God, then it too can be a stumbling block. When we become more involved in the 'romance' of worship, with the music, the form etc., rather than with God, it becomes a form of idolatry.

If we consider it more positively, God is bringing us to a place where our inner sustenance comes only from a relationship with the Lord Jesus Christ, rather than from any outward things. That which gives life a sense of meaning and purpose, that which gives us inner satisfaction and where we look for any kind of self-worth is to him alone.

Like the girl we may have a natural reticence to receive his affirmations, 'I am only a lily, common, not at all special . . . how can you love me so much?' That, itself, may be why we try so hard with the outer things, in an unconscious attempt to make ourselves something other than a common wild flower. But the love of our Saviour is to love us as we are. He sees a beauty in us which makes us a rose among brambles. We need to know and receive such affirmations and words of love deep in our spirits and break through the natural reluctance not to receive such words.

It seems that this deep receiving from God, rather than doing something outwardly for God, is where many of us hit a problem. In the recent renewal meetings where thousands have sought a deeper relationship with God, it seems to us that this is often a point of resistance yet also the point of breakthrough for many.

We were praying for a dear man during one of these meetings. He had been an evangelist for many years and had travelled a great distance to spend some nights in the renewal. We sensed that the Spirit of God was resting gently, yet powerfully upon him. We also sensed a resistance to receive the direction of the prayers God was giving us. It seemed God was simply loving him, pouring divine affirmation into his life. After a while we affirmed to the chap that the Spirit of God was upon him and that we could actually see the joy of the Lord upon his face. 'The Spirit of the Lord on me! Are you sure?' He was incredulous, as if this would happen to others but not to him. To us it was very clear. As the dear man moved into a place of deeply receiving what God was ministering to him, he quickly fell under the power of the Spirit and lay in God's presence for some while.

It has been like that for many. Christians are often 'doers', wanting to serve, wanting to work, rather than 'receivers' sitting before Jesus as he lovingly affirms us. A dear godly woman, who acts as spiritual director to many, expressed to Andy that God was leading her even further into a 'Mary' spirit of sitting and receiving. Naturally she would be a 'Martha', concerned, busy and sometimes fretful. God was doing a deeper work. In the body of Christ there is a preparation of those who are deeply lovers of Jesus.

'I only have eyes for you'

There is deep significance in the shepherd being attracted by the Shulammite's eyes. It speaks to us concerning the purity of our hearts, the singleness of our desires and direction. In two significant passages Jesus spoke about the eye: 'And if your eye causes you to stumble, tear it out and throw it away; it is better for you to enter life with one eye than to have two eyes and to be thrown into the hell of fire' (Mt 18:9). 'Your eye is the lamp of your body. If your eye is healthy, your whole body is full of light; but if it is not healthy, your body is full of darkness' (Lk 11:34).

The message, even the warning, is clear. Jesus wants us to be single in our hearts. There can be room for only one first and best love.

We had gathered together with a few close friends to pray. We had met with the express purpose of praying through the issue of a new home for our family. As we began to wait upon God, and to try to focus on the housing issue, the Lord came to us in a different way altogether. We could get no further than seeking his face and pleading with him for a deeper intimacy with himself.

This part of the Song was clearly brought to the group and a new appreciation and revelation was given. In a few precious moments the Lord drew near. We saw him with his protecting shadow, his sweet-tasting fruit, his loving intentions, his sustaining and refreshing and the wonder of his embrace as he touched us in the Spirit.

We had gathered to pray, perhaps with little more than a 'shopping list' of requests. He brought us to the banqueting house.

'Lord may our hearts be single in desiring you. To seek your face and not your hand. Reveal the depths of your love and tenderness.'

Note

[1] It may have been, in the culture of the day, at this point all

he could see were her eyes, as she remained veiled.

CHAPTER 5

COMFORT ZONES AND CALLING

In that blissful peacefulness of deep sleep a jarring, uncouth ringing pierced the quiet. After a few moments' disorientation it became clear: the phone was ringing. 'What time is it?', Andy muttered in a half groan. Jane was already to her feet and saying, 'Half past two!' as she made a hasty exit from the bedroom to stop the noise before it awoke the whole household.

'We've just had a domestic and there are two children needing a bed. Can you fix them up?', said the bright and cheery emergency social worker on the other end of the line. Jane's mind clicked into gear as, mentally, she moved the beds around and reorganised the home.

A couple of minutes later we were both wide awake, all thought of sleep rapidly disappearing as we rummaged as quietly as possible for bedding.

An hour later the phone rang again. 'It's OK. The emergency's over. Grandma has decided to take the kids home! Thanks for your trouble.'

Three thirty in the morning. We had willingly received the call to leave that beautiful, warm, snugly, comfort zone of sleep. Needless to say, we did not find it again that night.

Comfort zones are great places to be. Like a warm, quilted bed the comfort zone gives us a sense of well-being and security. We like to be there. But one of the principles of life is that for growth and development there is always the need to leave a comfort zone, to stretch further, to move on.

It is nearly always worth it, as the benefits of growth out-weigh the early discomfort. It is that initial 'leaving' which is the most difficult.

We both love to swim. Our fitness regime is to try to 'early bird' swim two or three times a week. In the summer, on warm days, there is nothing nicer than stripping off sweaty clothes and plunging into cool, refreshing water. In the winter it's different. You wrap up well to keep out the cold. The heater in the car is full on. The cold rain stings your face as you rush from the car to the swimming pool entrance. Taking off those warm clothes is hard! Getting into the water is even harder! But we know at the end of the swim, after 30 or so lengths, we will feel refreshed, exercised and ready to take on the world. Leaving the comfort zone of warm clothes to exercise is well worth it in the long run.

'Come away from your comfort zone'

The voice of my beloved!
Look, he comes,
leaping upon the mountains,
bounding over the hills.
My beloved is like a gazelle
or a young stag.
Look, there he stands
behind our wall,
gazing in at the windows,
looking through the lattice.
My beloved speaks and says to me:

'Arise, my love, my fair one,
and come away;
for now the winter is past,
the rain is over and gone.
The flowers appear on the earth;
the time of singing has come,
and the voice of the turtledove
is heard in our land.
The fig tree puts forth its figs,
and the vines are in blossom;
they give forth fragrance.

Arise, my love, my fair one,
  and come away.
O my dove, in the clefts of the rock,
  in the covert of the cliff,
let me see your face,
  let me hear your voice;
for your voice is sweet,
  and your face is lovely.
Catch us the foxes,
  the little foxes,
that ruin the vineyards –
  for our vineyards are in blossom.'

My beloved is mine and I am his;
  he pastures his flock among the lilies.
Until the day breathes
  and the shadows flee,
turn, my beloved, be like a gazelle
or a young stag on the cleft mountains.

Song 2:8–17

The last time we encountered the girl in the Song she was in the blissful contentment of being with her lover. While Solomon rested on his couch, the shepherd and shepherdess enjoyed a brief moment of love together. In his arms she was wonderfully safe, utterly fulfilled and aware only of the sweet savour of her lover.

In the way we are telling the story, however, this could not be the end. She is still in the tents of Solomon. Their love is not as yet consummated in marriage. There is a need of further movement towards each other.

In the nature of the book we are not given a timetable or anything like a strict chronology of their relationship. We are merely given snapshots. A snapshot of longing love in their separation; a snapshot of being together and truly enjoying one another. In this third section in the song the snapshot is one of movement. The shepherd wants to draw the Shulammite away.

It was, of course, her own cry in 1:4 'Draw me after you'. In her longing at that point she urged her shepherd lover to come and take her. This third section of the Song is a fulfilling of her wish. It's as if the shepherd has come to her and says, 'I have heard you. I have come. Now let's leave together. Springtime is here. There is no better time for you to come after me.'

In calling her, the shepherd utters wonderful affirmations of love. He calls her his 'beloved', his 'love', his 'fair one'. He longs for greater intimacy: 'Let me see your face, let me hear your voice; for your voice is sweet and your face is lovely'. Twice he urges her to 'arise' and follow him, and in the figure of 'catching the little foxes that ruin the vineyards' he urges her not to let anything prevent her from following.

This is, however, not one of her better moments! Despite his loving urgings and his gentle warnings she is unwilling to follow. She has arrived at a 'comfort zone'. She wants it to be just as it was in their last encounter. 'My beloved is mine and I am his' is a true statement of their relationship, but at this point she seems to want that relationship on her terms and not his. He urges her to arise and to follow and she wishes to stay and rest. Her exclamation, 'Turn, my beloved' is her way of saying 'I am not yet ready. Just at this point I cannot follow you in the way your want me to.'

It seems the shepherd does 'turn' and we find the girl alone upon her bed at night desperately needing her lover. So frantic is she, that she leaves the comfort of her tent and searches the city alone at night . . . but more of that in the next chapter.

Jesus 'behind our wall'

> Listen! I am standing at the door, knocking; if you hear my voice and open the door, I will come in to you and eat with you, and you with me.
>
> Rev 3:20

There is a sense in which our Saviour is always standing at the door. That is not to say that we do not enter into a deep intimacy with him, or that he is shut out permanently from our lives. In fact, perhaps the main reason that we have been drawn to the Song is that we *do* want to know him more closely than ever. We want to be able to say with real conviction 'I am my beloved's and he is mine!'

And yet, however close we are to him he remains eternal God; always more knowing than we can comprehend, always more pure than we can conceive, and always more powerful than we have yet imagined. It is because he is that kind of God that he is always seeking to draw us further, to stretch our capacity and comprehension. We think we have arrived, that we have learned something of him, that we know him intimately, and then we find that in truth he is 'behind our wall' and urging us again, 'Arise my love, my fair one, and come away'.

In Revelation, to the church at Laodicea, the picture is slightly different. There the Lord wants to *come in*, rather than urging his beloved to *follow him out*. But one element is the same. The Lord Jesus Christ is on the outside, one step removed from the believer, tantalisingly close, but still outside the door of his church.

In the evangelical tradition we have been used to leading people to Christ by 'asking him into your heart' and discipling people to believe that through the Spirit Christ is, indeed, on the inside of their lives. And of course, that is true. It is not a case of receiving Christ and losing him and receiving him and losing him. However, that teaching does shield us somewhat from the truth that there is always more of Jesus to know each day we live.

Here there is something of biblical paradox. While Jesus is in your heart because you are a believer, he is also standing outside of your heart urging you at times to open to let him in further, or else urging you to follow him out and away from your comfort zone.

In this portion of the Song, the picture given to us is of a Saviour who has been with us in intimate embrace, who has spoken wonderfully affirming words of love deep in our spirits, and yet who now wants to draw us still further away from everything we know as safe and comfortable and towards himself. We want to stay in the intimacy of personal embrace. He wants us to leap and skip with him on the hills.

It is a cycle of life. Intimacy, followed by challenge to arise, followed by willing obedience leading to greater intimacy.

Good things become substitutes

There is within the human psyche a deep need to find a place of security. Most of us feel more at ease when we have an inner feeling of safety, than when we are out on a limb in some new, untried venture. Even those who love the thrill of the new, those dear pioneering spirits, still like the 'fireside' to retreat to. And that is the way God made us. We were made to be safe and secure. However, our security is to be in his purpose for us, trusting him as little children, knowing that while we trust him, we are safe.

But sometimes the good things of God, things that God has given to us, themselves become where we are safe rather than in God himself. In other words, the good things of God, from our past encounters with him, become for us a comfort zone. That's OK for a while, but our beloved shepherd will come to us with his disturbing words, 'Arise my love, and come away.' There is always more.

We have observed that some children who are deprived of good, stable, loving, parenting tend to find 'comfort' in good things, but in inappropriate ways. For instance, for these children, food can become a substitute for love. Love has been denied and so something else is found to provide comfort. Food is perhaps the only certainty these children have known and so the child's relationship with food and her eating habits become distorted. Greed, overeating and storing food in little hideaways is common. That which is good, in this case food, has become a substitute for parental love which has never been present. To 'wean' a child away from this kind of distortion and towards a proper relationship with food can be quite difficult, for the child has developed a comfort zone and will feel threatened if you try to lead her from it.

Leading a child through such a 'disturbance' can be quite painful. We know it is for her own good, but we still feel for her disorientation and sense of loss as we move her from a valued comfort zone.

There is a clear analogy with spiritual life. God has given us so many good things. One of our difficulties is that we can become reliant on those 'things' and make them into a substitute for God himself.

The little things that spoil

It seems that the shepherd is aware of her uncertainty and hesitancy. In a loving and gentle way he warns the Shulammite about 'little foxes' which spoil the vines. He is speaking of those little things which creep in unbeknown to us and do immense damage.

In the spirit, those little foxes are many. They can be God's good gifts, distorted into being what they were never meant to be. They may be past experiences of God which we rely on in the present, though the power and immediacy of God has left them. The little foxes may be fears to move on because of the uncertainty of the future. They may be those sins which entangle us and distract us from God. All these little foxes bind us to themselves and distract us from the pure love of our shepherd.

Here are two examples of 'little foxes' as good gifts which become substitutes for God which affect many.

The first relates to church. Church is without a doubt God's plan for his people. We were never meant to be alone. There is to be the two or three gathered in Jesus' name to bind and loose. There are to be times of gathering to worship God and together to share in the Apostles' teaching, prayer, fellowship and the breaking of bread.

However, without a doubt, church can and often does become the greatest substitute for the true and deep knowledge of God. It becomes familiar to us. As Christians we make it into our strongest comfort zone. With the multiplicity of churches we search around until we find one which suits our personality and worship preferences. We then make it our own and learn to 'wear it' like a pair of old Levi's. Woe betide anyone who tries to take away our comfort zone! Those who have tried under God to lead a church through the painful process of renewal will have heard expressed in a myriad of different ways, 'We like it this way. We've never done that before. I don't like the new songs . . . Bible, chairs, building, worship style, pastor, way the offering is taken, flavour of wine in the communion chalice . . . ' The list is endless!

Sadly, it is not only related to taking an 'old' church into renewal. In a short time that which was fresh, new and alive with the Spirit of God becomes the latest comfort zone. Moving those once renewed into fresh renewal is sometimes harder than raising the dead! Church, forms, structures, both traditional and charismatic, often become a substitute for knowing the shepherd.

Many Christians have the experience of church life when the forms, and activities, even church itself, becomes a substitute for Christ. 'I wish I had more time to pray on a Sunday morning, but I had to prepare for the children's work.' That which was initially good has become a little fox which actually destroys the vine.

The second example is that for God's called and anointed leaders, their ministries often become the little fox which spoils the vineyard. Ministries are never set in granite. God gives them, blesses them, but calls them further, changes them and from time to time ends them. Leaders have a tendency to hold on tight, possess their ministries and make them into a substitute for moving deeper into God. One of the tragedies of participating in many leaders' meetings is watching leaders jockeying for position, protecting their 'turf' and being consumed with 'my ministry'. For many, ministry has become a substitute for knowing God.

The little foxes are also those fears which beset us when

we are called to some new moving with God.

> He said, 'Come.' So Peter got out of the boat, started walking on the water, and came toward Jesus. But when he noticed the strong wind, he became frightened, and beginning to sink, he cried out, 'Lord, save me!'
>
> Mt 14:29–30

The disciples had just seen Jesus feed the 5,000 and had seen something of his wonder and power. Following this wonderful event, they were sent to the other side of the lake in a boat, while Jesus remained in the mountains to pray.

Early in the morning, they saw Jesus walking towards them and Peter, seemingly full of faith, asked if he could come to Jesus on the water. In response to Jesus, Peter did begin to walk on water, but immediately the little foxes came in. Peter noticed the strong winds. He became frightened and began to sink. But that was not the end of the story. Jesus held out his hand and Peter was safe. The result was more faith and more worship for the disciples.

The shepherd calls us from the comfort zone of our boat. We willingly follow; the little foxes of fear arise and we begin to sink. Yet Jesus is always there. If he calls, the truth is that he will always enable us to do that which he asks. Just watch out for the foxes. The result will be a drawing closer, more faith and more worship.

Turn, leave me just now

In the Song the girl had heard the shepherd calling her onward. She had received much love from her beloved. However, she had turned her experiences into a comfort zone. The call to arise is full of discomfort for her.

She confesses 'My beloved is mine and I am his', which is a true statement of their love. The problem is that she expresses it in a negative way. It is as if she says, 'We belong to each other, but please don't call me to come away with you. I want to stay in the warmth of your embrace. Don't ask me to follow you leaping on the mountains and bounding upon the hills.' She wants to remain in her comfort zone. He calls her away, but she says 'turn . . . leave me just now.' What a tragedy that is at this point in the story! She does not follow him and soon finds herself bereft of his presence. The irony is that her comfort zone no longer provided comfort to her.

This lesson is one to learn again and again. It is something we will face many times in our walk with Jesus. He will often call us onward into new aspects of relationship with himself.

Saturday morning, 17th August 1991, 5.20 am. We had been praying all through the night, seeking God over some important issues. At this point Andy was on his own in his office and God spoke clearly. 'Andy, I require the sacrifice of Isaac.' It was a very brief, very clear moment. Isaac was the ministry and although God had clearly given it, he now required it back. Andy wept.

It was too much. The ministry had become for Andy a comfort zone and actually was in danger of becoming a little fox. In the days that followed, confusing voices clouded the clarity of the voice of God. Andy held on to the ministry. To a degree there remained blessing, but the intensity of spiritual anointing was lost. In just over two years that particular ministry was taken from him.

That Saturday morning encounter with God was followed by a period characterised in the words of the Shulammite: 'Upon my bed at night I sought him whom my soul loves, I sought him . . . but found him not.'

The message is clear. When the beloved shepherd calls us to arise, to leave the comfort zone, then ready following is always the better way.

CHAPTER 6

SEARCHING IN THE CITY

When our children were smaller a favourite game was 'hide and seek'. Each holiday time we would try to find a new exciting place to play our games. One favourite place was the old priory on the Holy Island of Lindisfarne. Holy Island has been a special place for Christians for centuries. English Christianity was birthed on this wild and windswept piece of land. Miracles were believed to have taken place at the shrine of St. Cuthbert, and Lindisfarne became a place of pilgrimage for many. We have spent many happy holidays there. The priory is a lovely enclosed place with just one gate in and out, with lots of little nooks and crannies in its crumbling stone walls. It's a first-rate place for a good game of hide and seek, though we have wondered what the old monks would have made of us!

One day while playing, we failed to find Rebekah. She was then about five years old and we became exceedingly worried. We soon started to look for her, shouting her name repeatedly and running around the priory with increasing anxiety. She remained unfound and our searching became more and more frantic and desperate. We started to ask people, 'Have you seen our little girl?' We described her clothing, her height, her hair-style and all else we could remember. By now there was a sense of urgency in us all. Had anything happened to her? Would we see her again?

Happily, about 20 minutes later (which seemed like a lifetime) we found her. She was waiting patiently in a tiny nook in the wall, still playing the game, and feeling really proud that she had beaten us all. In her little shelter our cries had gone unheard and our efforts to find her unseen. Oh the feelings of joy and relief! Needless to say, that ended our game and we didn't let her out of our sight again that day.

In the Song, though in different circumstances, the Shulammite faced a period of loss and searching.

> *Upon my bed at night*
> *   I sought him whom my soul loves;*
> *I sought him, but found him not;*
> *   I called him, but he gave no answer.*
> *'I will rise now and go about the city,*
> *   in the streets and in the squares;*
> *I will seek him whom my soul loves.'*
> *   I sought him, but found him not.*
> *The sentinels found me,*
> *   as they went about in the city.*
> *'Have you seen him whom my soul loves.'*
> *Scarcely had I passed them,*
> *   when I found him whom my soul loves.*
> *I held him, and would not let him go*
> *   until I brought him into my mother's house,*
> *   and into the chamber of her that conceived me.*
> *I adjure you, O daughter of Jerusalem,*
> *   by the gazelles or the wild does:*
> *do not stir up or awaken love*
> *   until it is ready!*

Song 3:1–5

The girl, challenged to leave her comfort zone, had replied to the shepherd 'Turn, leave me, I am not yet ready'. The shepherd left her. His call was dependent on her willingness to follow, and at this point there was an unwillingness on her part. It was not that she did not love him, but simply that she had become comfortable in the king's tents.

Her comfort zone, however, no longer provided the place of comfort she had experienced previously. In her loss she comes to a new realisation. She will now leave her comfort zone in a desperate bid to find her lover.

In the girl, at this point, we observe the same kind of urgency that we felt when we had lost Rebekah. Her searching has a frantic feel about it. She leaves her comfortable bed, runs out into the city, combs the streets, searches in the square in a desperate bid to find the shepherd lover.[1] She asks in desperation 'Have you seen him whom my soul loves?'

Suddenly, she finds him and exclaims in utter relief that she will hold him for ever and not let him go.

Searching for Jesus

In our Christian lives we can find ourselves in the same predicament as the girl. There are times when we lose all sight and sense of our beloved. Most Christians know times when it seems Jesus has withdrawn. Love for him is not less, but any sense of his closeness is missing. Intimacy is absent.

Now there are chiefly two ways that this felt presence and sense of intimacy can be lost. The more difficult one to understand is when, for his own purposes, Jesus withdraws himself from us. We are not conscious of any disobedience nor recognised sin, and yet we lose all sense of the nearness of Jesus. It has been called 'the dark night of the soul' in some literature.

The second main way we lose the sense of Jesus is when we have walked another way, when we have turned from him and excluded him in some way or another.

It is in this second predicament that we find the girl in the Song. We will discover that she does endure 'the dark night of the soul', but at a later point in the story.

The shepherd has called her to leave her comfort zone. She has responded negatively. He has withdrawn from her. Her desperation is a result of her unwillingness to follow where he has called. In one way, this period in her relationship with the shepherd could have been avoided, if only she had been willing. Thankfully, for our sake, it is included in the story because often we are so much like the Shulammite. Our Saviour calls us onward. Sometimes we respond willingly, joyfully and immediately. Other times we have become comfortable; we hesitate, and our reluctance is followed by the loss of the sense of his presence.

Some years ago we had a very real experience of this. God had shown us a vision, a way forward which would have demanded a great exercise of faith. We didn't follow. There were many good reasons we hesitated: it may have caused problems in the church we were leading at the time, perhaps people would be hurt, perhaps we would cause a split. Some people shared the vision with us, and others were more hesitant. We decided to wait a while. It is not our place to speak for others involved. But in waiting we personally lost the intimacy with Jesus we had been enjoying. It was a very uncomfortable time.

The positive side of such experiences is that in them God causes an even deeper longing for renewed intimacy. For us the finding of intimacy again has come in the time of refreshing. In restoring us God has given us the realisation that closeness with him is something we don't want to lose again. As far as is possible, and whatever the cost, we have made a commitment to follow where he leads, to arise when he calls.

Called to enter the land

The principle is clearly seen a number of times in the Scriptures. God had called the children of Israel to enter the land he had prepared for them. Spies were sent to look over the land. Of the twelve who were sent, only two, Joshua and Caleb, could see the great potential of a land 'flowing with milk and honey'. The other ten had become comfortable in their wanderings.

> Then the men who had gone up with him said, 'We are not able to go up against this people, for they are stronger than we.' So they brought to the Israelites an unfavourable report of the land that they had spied out, saying, 'The land that we have gone through as spies is a land that devours its inhabitants; and all the people that we saw

in it are of great size. There we saw the Nephilim (the Anakites come from the Nephilim); and to ourselves we seemed like grasshoppers, and so we seemed to them.' Then all the congregation raised a loud cry, and the people wept that night. And all the Israelites complained against Moses and Aaron; the whole congregation said to them, 'Would that we had died in the land of Egypt! Or would that we had died in this wilderness!'

Num 13:31:14:2

The people wanted to stay in a safe place and to be fed with manna and quails. The result was forty years in the wilderness. After forty years and much desperation, when Joshua finally led the people into the good land, their response was much different. They answered Joshua: 'All that you have commanded us we will do, and wherever you send us we will go' (Josh 1:16). They said to Joshua, 'Truly the LORD has given all the land into our hands; moreover all the inhabitants of the land melt in fear before us' (Josh 2:24).

Their experience of the wilderness had brought them to a desperate place where to know God in his ways was the most important issue for them. Where once they had faltered, now they followed willingly.

Losing the presence through deliberate sin

Deliberate sin, more than any other issue, causes us to lose the sweet presence of the Saviour. As we grow towards holiness, God will reveal areas of our lives which are incompatible with his purity and goodness. It is revealed as something we are engaged in, or some course of action that we have decided upon which causes our spirits to be disturbed. It may well be something in which we have found pleasure in the past, which has previously not caused us problems. But at a certain point, as we are growing closer to him, God shows us his will. Our response is sometimes 'No, Lord!' (a bit of a contradiction in terms!), and he allows us that freedom.

The Lord does not force himself upon us. He will more often than not simply withdraw his presence, gently slipping away until we are desperate and willing to say 'Yes, Lord!'

Care does need to be exercised here. We are not suggesting that anything is acceptable until we have a direct revelation from God. In some areas we do not need a 'personal word', for God has made his way very clear already. In these areas we need to pay particular attention to the clear teaching of the Scriptures. God will never go against his written word. From time to time we have counselled a young woman or man who has fallen in love with a non-Christian. Their cry is often, 'But I love him/her. God hasn't told me it's wrong.' Of course not, God has already made his will known in this area: 'Do not be mismatched with unbelievers. For what partnership is there between righteousness and lawlessness? Or what fellowship is there between light and darkness?' (2 Cor 6:14).

It might seem harsh to the young people very much in love, but God's ways are always wisest and best. Where such a relationship continues, in nearly all cases the believer loses their vitality, and their walk with God is compromised. In such cases there is no need for a personal word from God. He has already given a general word to all of us.

Even David, a man after God's own heart, fell into sin and lost the presence of God. His sin in 2 Samuel 11–12, in the complicity in the murder of Uriah and the taking of his wife, Bathsheba, resulted in the most awful period of the loss of God's nearness. Sin and the felt presence of God are not compatible. David's case is a warning to all of us that however far we feel we have walked with God, we may still fall. With the remaining sin in our hearts there is yet deceit into which we can fall. Even in the great saint of God, to take the way of willfulness and rebellion against God will result in the loss of his presence.

God's provision of the desperate heart

In David's case, when the sin was revealed there was such a desperation in him to find God again. This is most clearly described in Psalm 51, which we understand was written when the prophet Nathan pointed out his sin. It stands for us as one of the most poignant parts of all the Scriptures. David's longing to know God's presence again breathes through the whole psalm.

It is God's goodness to us that creates within us such a desperation when we lose the sense of his presence. Like the girl in the Song, we will always be brought to the inner frantic feeling of desperate searching. It is God's provision, for it is there in the searching that we find him. Jesus gave us a clue towards this in his teaching on the Spirit.

> So I say to you, Ask, and it will be given you; search, and you will find; knock, and the door will be opened for you. For everyone who asks receives, and everyone who searches finds, and for everyone who knocks, the door will be opened. Is there anyone among you who, if your child asks for a fish, will give a snake instead of a fish? Or if the child asks for an egg, will give a scorpion? If you then, who are evil, know how to give good gifts to your children, how much more will the heavenly Father give the Holy Spirit to those who ask him!
>
> Lk 11:9–13

There are so many good things in this teaching. For our purposes it is the sense of asking, searching and knocking which is important. Without that sense of urgency and longing for more, it is unlikely that we will really know the depths of God.

For most of us, naturally there is a great deal of lethargy in spiritual things. The greatest disease among God's people is their apathy in the deep things of God. We are simply not desperate enough. It is often God allowing us to pass through a dry time with a sense of loss which produces in us that sense of frantic desperation.

In the renewal that many experienced in the Autumn/Winter of 1994, there were many testimonies to a period of desperation in which the apathy and lethargy of many was turned to almost reckless longing. It seems that God prepared many for the outpouring of his Spirit by creating in them a searching heart.

In finding him is a greater joy and depth of love. We have heard recently, night after night in the renewal meetings, of people from all walks of life and all ages who have given testimony to periods of desperate searching, ending in finding their shepherd. Their stories are all different, with many different details, but all end in the experience of a closer relationship with God.

The way of the searching heart

Frantic searching is not always the most ordered of activities, nor is it always carried out in the wisest of ways. Searching in the wrong way can end in frustration. With David we cry out to God 'Restore to me the joy of your salvation', yet he seems elusive. The girl in the Song sought earnestly and asked the 'sentinels' of the city if they had seen the shepherd. There is the feeling in the poem that she would have tried anything to find him.

For some time Christians have been seeking Jesus in many ways. We have asked of the 'sentinels' where we might find our shepherd. In this generation we have more Christian conferences, books, tapes and videos than ever before. Resources for understanding God and his ways have never been greater. We have the Scriptures in literally dozens of translations and paraphrases. Yet, still many of us have been dry, and our searching in those areas has not resulted in the presence of the Saviour. The answer may be simple and from the lips of Jesus himself: 'You search the scriptures because you think that in them you have eternal life; and it is they that testify on my behalf. Yet you refuse to come to me to have life' (Jn 5:39–40).

We have never in history had more help to search the Scriptures. But the Scriptures by themselves do not satisfy the longing of the human heart. The Bible is to point us to Jesus that we might come to him and, in him, find our intimacy and meaning. It might sound like 'heresy' to suggest it, but what is needed in the church at present is not more teaching, Bible study, and understanding, but simply more of Jesus. To know the Scriptures is good, but it is not a substitute for knowing the Saviour in a direct way, deep in our spirits.

It is not the benefit of more knowledge, or the thrill of the 'great conference', nor listening to 'solid and sound' teaching, but the direct and personal knowing of Jesus which our generation needs. May we be willing to let go of anything and everything that we might take hold of him alone.

Note

[1] This is another incident in the Song which leads us to interpret the lover as a shepherd rather than the king. It is unlikely that the girl would search the city streets and squares to find the king of Israel.

CHAPTER 7

LOVE'S TEMPTATION

What is that coming up from the wilderness,
    like a column of smoke,
perfumed with myrrh and frankincense,
    with all the fragrant powders of the merchant?
Look, it is the litter of Solomon!
    Around it are sixty mighty men of the mighty men of Israel,
all equipped with swords
    and expert in war,
each with his sward at his thigh
because of alarms by night.
King Solomon made himself a palanquin
    from the wood of Lebanon.
He made its posts of silver,
    its back of gold, its seat of purple;
its interior was inlaid with love.
    Daughters of Jerusalem, come out.
Look, O daughters of Zion,
    at King Solomon,
at the crown with which his mother crowned him
    on the day of his wedding,
    on the day of the gladness of his heart.

Song 3:6–11

We always feel that there should be a loud fanfare at this point in the story. Something noisy and bright is happening. Most of the other scenes in the Song are either soliloquies, or else dialogues between the two lovers or the few other characters in the poem. Here, all tranquillity and intimacy is broken as we are invited to look upon Solomon's wealth and splendour as he approaches Jerusalem with all the trappings of monarchy.

Some years ago we took a break to 'see the sights of London'. Living in the country we always enjoy life in the capital (for a brief while at least!). We were meandering in St. James Park, having spent the morning at Tussauds and the Planetarium. Our legs were tired and we were looking for an empty bench when we heard the sound of a marching band. We realised quickly that the Brigade of Guards were parading down the Mall. For all we knew, perhaps the Queen or a member of the Royal Family would be with them? Despite aching legs, and the odd complaint from one of the little ones with us, we hastily half jogged, half ran across the park. What a spectacle! Soldiers immaculately turned out in red tunics, black bearskins and shining instruments. On this occasion the guards were unaccompanied by royalty, but the sense of excitement and anticipation could be felt in all the crowd as we watched them march by. It must have been like that for the inhabitants of Jerusalem when Solomon paraded with his retinue. Vibrant, colourful, exciting . . .

But this was not merely a royal procession. It refers to the royal wedding of Solomon. Solomon had married 700 times to women of royal birth beside his 300 concubines (1 Kings 11:3), and it is unlikely that there was such a magnificent parade each time. It's most likely, therefore, that this refers to Solomon's marriage to the princess of Egypt (1 Kings 3:1), a highly significant marriage with major political implications. Quite clearly, such a royal spectacle could not refer to the king's marriage to a rustic shepherd girl from Shunem. Its place within the Song is there for other purposes.[1]

At the end of the last section of the Song the shepherdess had found her beloved and was just approaching the deepest point of their intimacy to date. When she asserts, 'I brought him into my mother's house, and into the chamber of her that conceived me', we realise that the two lovers are nearing the point of the consummation of their relationship.

If we were writing the poem we would probably have moved directly to the beginning of chapter 4. The girl's desire is the further and deeper love of the shepherd. That desire is fulfilled in chapter 4. It follows quite naturally.

But here, all of a sudden, there is this interruption and we are not expecting it. From the safety and intimacy of the shepherd's arms to the great fanfare as Solomon enters Jerusalem, in the space of one verse. It is a jarring interruption to the intimacy of love and provides for the girl a further temptation.

It is unlikely that we have a direct sequential movement from the shepherd's intimacy to the marriage of Solomon and the Egyptian princess. It is probably a literary device to present a contrast for us. The pure love of shepherd and shepherdess is placed next to the pomp and show of a royal wedding, the context of which was Solomon's flagrant disobedience to Yahweh, God of Israel. It was Solomon's foreign wives who turned him away from true religion (1 Kings 11:1–8).

The Shulammite, in her turn, had already shunned the life of the harem with all its advantages and luxuries. She had turned down the kudos of being one who belonged to Solomon . . . all because she knew the pure love of the shepherd. Now here, at her place of intimacy, having confessed her love in the strongest way, that nothing will ever separate her from the shepherd, the old temptation emerges again, yet this time in the strongest form. Solomon, upon his palanquin, surrounded by his elite guard. . .and she could have been with him! He had wanted her. She had to this point resisted. Would she continue to stand strong in her true love?

How like our own Christian relationship this is! The Song at this point speaks powerfully to us. We often discover that place of deep contentment with the Lord, only to find that almost immediately temptation comes to try and distract us.

The grass if always greener . . .

Happily, in our story in the Song the shepherd girl does not follow the temptation. At the beginning of the next portion we find her still in that place of oneness with the shepherd.

However, temptation will nearly always present itself as something bigger or better or more attractive than that which we already have. Temptation is not usually bad in itself, in fact the object of temptation is often a good thing, but is always something which seeks to take us away from that place of unspoiled fellowship. Certainly, in the description of the king approaching Jerusalem we can see only good. It must have been an amazing spectacle to watch. But for the girl in the Song it presented a temptation.

The story of the first temptation in the Bible is probably familiar to us all. Adam and Eve were in the most perfect place. God was supplying their every need and they were in perfect, fulfiling communion with him. They spent time in an intimate relationship with God, where he came to them and talked and walked with them. Sometimes 'familiarity breeds contempt' and it is good to look again at the familiar. We often see new things that way.

> Now the serpent was more crafty than any other wild animal that the LORD God had made. He said to the woman, 'Did God say, 'You shall not eat from any tree in the garden?' The woman said to the serpent, 'We may eat of the fruit of the trees in the garden; but God said, 'You shall not eat of the fruit of the tree that is in the middle of the garden, nor shall you touch it, or you shall die.' But the serpent said to the woman, 'You will not die; for God knows that when you eat of it your eyes will be opened, and you will be like God, knowing good and evil.' So when the woman saw that the tree was good for food, and that it was a delight to the eyes, and that the tree was to be desired to make one wise, she took of its fruit and ate; and she also gave some to her husband, who was with her, and he ate.
>
> Gen 3:1–6

The serpent tempted Adam and Eve with something that at first looked better than what they had. The prospect of having knowledge, of knowing even as God does, even to be like

God, seemed to be a better option than that place where they experienced dependent and loving intimacy with God. Unfortunately, they succumbed to the temptation, with the terrible consequence of loss of intimate fellowship with God (Gen 3:23–24). They found to their cost, and ours, that the grass was not greener on the other side. The 'better' prospect of knowledge, with its accompanying loss of innocence could not replace the intimate knowledge of God. It looked better, it appeared attractive, but it couldn't deliver its promise.

Jane was talking to our neighbours recently, a lovely Christian couple whom we have known for some years. Both David and Susan believed that God had spoken to them and called them to another part of the country where a new Christian work was beginning. David had been seeking employment for some time and they were sure God had shown them which town and which fellowship they were to be part of. In God's goodness a job opened in the new area which was just right for David and we rejoiced with them. However, as soon as the job opened, David was immediately telephoned and asked to consider a better job elsewhere. It became a major temptation for them. God had clearly spoken, they were happily walking closely with him and yet something seemingly better arose. Happily, they recognised this as the distraction and temptation it surely was and followed the prompting of God.

Temptation is not sin

It's also important to understand that the temptation is, in itself, not sinful. Even Jesus was tempted, yet we know that he had no sin. We read that Jesus had just been baptised by John, the heavens had opened and the Father had made that wonderful declaration, 'You are my son, the beloved; with you I am well pleased'.

The Father speaks of his delight in the Son, he makes a public declaration and affirmation of their intimacy. Surely, this is a place which reveals the greatest mutual appreciation of each other. Then we read that immediately the Spirit drove him into the wilderness to be tempted.

There is, thus, in the life and example of the Saviour a close connection between a depth of intimacy and temptation to leave that intimacy for something else. Having enjoyed and heard the declaration of intimacy between Father and Son, the Son is tested, tempted to leave the will of the Father to engage in other things.

Undoubtedly they were very strong and presented a clear challenge to Jesus. To be temptations there must have been the possibility that at that point Jesus could have fallen. In the same way that in the Garden of Gethsemane Jesus agonised over the Father's will. Both circumstances presented immense challenges to Jesus. Would he give in or remain trusting in the Father? Thankfully, Jesus overcame and in both situations glory came to God. After the wilderness the ministry of Jesus began in earnest; after Gethsemane the way was clear to the cross.

We do need to be aware that temptation only becomes sin when we allow it to become so.

> Blessed is anyone who endures temptation. Such a one has stood the test and will receive the crown of life that the Lord has promised to those who love him. No one, when tempted, should say, 'I am being tempted by God'; for God cannot be tempted by evil and he himself tempts no one. But one is tempted by one's own desire, being lured and enticed by it; then, when that desire has conceived, it gives birth to sin, and that sin, when it is fully grown, gives birth to death. Do not be deceived, my beloved.
>
> James 1:12–16

The temptations to Jesus in the wilderness were to leave the intimate place of trust in the Father and to find other means of provision, significance and protection. But Jesus did not allow the temptations to lead him into sin.

It is in these specific areas that we too will find causes of temptation. In God's goodness we are to find all of our provision, sense of destiny and security in himself alone. It is in those areas that we grow as we develop intimacy with Christ. Much of life is taken up with the worries of how we will manage, what significance our life is to have, and whether we will find safety as we try to do it. As we grow in love for Christ, all of these things are taken care of as we trust in him. We do not need to look elsewhere. The temptation will be to meet those needs ourselves.

A friend of ours once came to us having a problem with temptation. She loved her husband and family dearly, but recently was being completely distracted by a new man at the supermarket where she worked. She was at a stage in her life when she wondered what the significance of it all was. The temptation for her was that through the attentions of this man, and through the possibility of pleasing him, she would find some significance to her life which was at that point eluding her.

She told us that she had become very attracted to him and was spending a lot of time trying to think of ways to be near him. Happily, she had recognised that this was not right for her and asked for our help, which we willingly gave. We prayed that as God had brought this temptation into the light that its power would be broken. In God's goodness, its power was broken and, after confession and prayer for our friend, the temptation no longer existed.

There will be many occasions of temptation which will seek to move us from a position of trust to one of seeking some other way to meet our needs of provision, significance and safety. At the back of temptation is often lack of trust. God has promised from the lips of Jesus that all our needs will be met – if we seek first his kingdom. Eugene Peterson paraphrases Matthew 6 in a very interesting and memorable way:

> If God gives such attention to the appearance of wildflowers – most of which are never ever seen – don't you think he'll attend to you, take pride in you, do his best for you? What I'm trying to do is get you to relax, to not be so preoccupied with *getting*, so you can respond to God's *giving*. People who don't know God and the way

he works fuss over these things, but you both know God and how he works. Steep your life in God-reality, God-initiative, God-provisions. Don't worry about missing out. You'll find all your everyday human concerns will be met.

Give your entire attention to what God is doing right now, and don't get worked up about what may or may not happen tomorrow. God will help you deal with whatever hard things come up when the time comes.[2]

One of the insidious ways that temptation works is to cause us to worry and to scheme how we might make things work out ourselves. Even if we do not allow the temptation to lead us into sin, it can often lead us into anxiously worrying. It robs us of peace. Learning to grow in intimacy with the shepherd will save us hours of worry and many sleepless nights.

The green grass of Christian service

'The grass is always greener on the other side' rarely proves true. The temptation is usually to look over the fence at what appears to be greener grass.

Jack Deere has written a 'landmark' book with regard to the work of the Spirit.[3] Dr. Deere was a seminary professor in a conservative school before, in the 1980s, receiving a new perspective on the work of the Spirit in believers' lives.

Towards the end of his book he keys into the theme of the Song of Songs and passion for God. From his experience he tells us that it is possible for many things, good things, to become a temptation to the 'greener' side. He comments:

> What I'm saying is that it is possible to put almost any good thing above Jesus Christ without realising what we are doing. We can put the Bible and its commandments above the Lord. We can put spiritual gifts and even various kinds of worship above the Lord. We can put various forms of ministry – witnessing, caring for the poor, praying for the sick – above the Lord. It is possible to be seduced by any of those things.[4]

Notice the word Dr. Deere uses – *seduce*. That is the language of temptation. We do need to be careful. More of any of those things does not necessarily mean we are growing in intimacy with Jesus. In fact, any of them may become a temptation to seduce us away from developing intimacy with him.

Notes

[1] For a more detailed treatment of this see Tom Gledhill, *The Message of the Song of Songs*, (IVP: Leicester, 1994), pp 149–152.

[2] Eugene H. Peterson, *The Message*, (NavPress: Colorado Springs, 1993), p 21.

[3] Jack Deere, *Surprised by the Power of the Spirit*, (Zondervan: Grand Rapids, 1993), British Edition, (Kingsway: Eastbourne, 1994).

[4] *Ibid*, p 191.

CHAPTER 8

THE CONSUMMATION OF LOVE

The shepherd girl has longed for her shepherd lover. She has tasted something of his intimacy. She has known the pain of separation and the joy of renewed love. She has overcome the enormous temptation of Solomon's wealth and glory and the scene is set for the wedding celebration. Her desire of 3:4, 'I brought him into my mother's house, and into the chamber of her that conceived me', is wonderfully fulfilled in chapter 4 of the Song. The young girl, so very much in love with her shepherd, at last becomes the bride.

In the first part of this section of the Song we find the shepherd speaking intimate words of love and then finally proposing to the girl. While in earlier sections the words of the shepherd's love have been few and measured, at this point he gives voice to his passionate love for his bride. It is quite possible that he sees her unveiled for the first time and he is smitten with her beauty.

> How beautiful you are, my love,
>   how very beautiful!
> Your eyes are doves
>   behind your veil.
> Your hair is like a flock of goats,
>   moving down the slopes of Gilead.
> Your teeth are like a flock of shorn ewes
>   that have come up from the washing,
> all of which bear twins,
>   and not one among them is bereaved.

> Your lips are like a crimson thread,
>   and your mouth is lovely.
> Your cheeks are like halves of a pomegranate
>   behind your veil.
> Your neck is like the tower of David,
>   built in courses;
> on it hang a thousand bucklers,
>   all of them shields of warriors.
> Your two breasts are like two fawns,
>   twins of a gazelle,
>   that feed among the lilies.

                                    Song 4:1–5

Her answer to the shepherd, this time, is different to that of chapter 2, where in response to his desire for her to 'arise and come away with me', she responds with 'turn my beloved'. At that point in their relationship she was not ready for the fuller commitment of the marriage covenant. However, through process of time and circumstances she is now ready. Her response is counterpoint to her words of chapter 2.

> *Until the day breathes*
>   *and the shadows flee,*
> *I will hasten to the mountain of myrrh*
>   *and the hill of frankincense.*

                                    Song 4:6

Her positive affirmations of love are followed by the shepherd's further overtures of marriage:

> You are altogether beautiful, my love;
>   there is no flaw in you.
> Come with me from Lebanon, my bride;
>   come with me from Lebanon.
> Depart from the peak of Amana,
>   from the peak of Senir and Hermon,
> from the dens of lions,
>   from the mountains of leopards.

                                    Song 4:7–8

What follows is for many commentators a description of their wedding night, when love is consummated for the first time. We are introduced to the scene by the words of the bridegroom as we are given an insight into the intimacy of their love. Until this point he has called her his love, his fair one. The tenor of the poem changes now as six times in this section he refers to the Shulammite as 'my bride'. The longings of their love find full expression, as at last their courtship finds completion in marital love. We allow the newly weds to speak for themselves.

You have ravished my heart, my sister, my bride,
    you have ravished my heart with a glance of your eyes,
        with one jewel of your necklace.
How sweet is your love, my sister, my bride!
    how much better is your love than wine,
        and the fragrance of your oils than any spice!
Your lips distil nectar, my bride;
    honey and milk are under your tongue;
        the scent of your garments is like the scent of Lebanon.
A garden locked is my sister, my bride,
    a garden locked, a fountain sealed.
Your channel is an orchard of pomegranates
    with all choicest fruits,
        henna with nard,
nard and saffron, calamus and cinnamon,
    with all trees of frankincense, myrrh and aloes,
with all chief spices-
a garden fountain, a well of living water,
    and flowing streams from Lebanon.

Awake, O north wind,
    and come, O south wind!
Blow upon my garden
    that its fragrance may be wafted abroad.
Let my beloved come to his garden,
    and eat its choicest fruits.

I come to my garden, my sister, my bride;
I gather my myrrh with my spice,
I eat my honeycomb with my honey,
I drink my wine with my milk.
Eat, friends, drink.
    and be drunk with love.

Song 4:9–5:1

For those with eyes to see, the interchange between bride-groom and bride is a delicate and a beautiful description of their wedding night and there is much for us to learn in this scene. There are words of unparalleled sweetness as we glimpse their most intimate of nights.

At a natural level, it emphasises for us the sacredness, purity and beauty of sexual intercourse. However, in its positive affirmations of human sexuality the passage urges us to see that sexual intimacy needs to be saved for the covenant of marriage. Though there had been expression of love in word, caress and longing during their courtship, sexual intercourse had been reserved for this night and those which followed it. It is not that they were unaware of their sexuality before their marriage. Far from it! The courtship scenes resonate with sexual feeling. It would be wrong, as some unfortunately do, to advise young people to deny their sexuality in the sense of trying to eradicate it. We are all sexual beings. Before marriage, however, that sexuality is to be recognised, but controlled and saved. Young people need to be taught to thank God for their sexuality. The physical expression of their sexuality in intercourse is reserved for the night of their marriage. The very act of becoming one flesh is not a light or haphazard thing, not a thing of experimentation. It is a sacred joining together, a bonding like no other in human relationships. Sexual intercourse is to be reserved for marriage.

The shepherd tells us this in an oblique way when he refers to his bride as a beautiful and abundant garden. But it is a garden which is as yet locked, a fountain which is as yet sealed. Through a delicate figure of speech he is referring to her purity and virginity.

In her turn she is not merely an object of use but readily and willingly responds to his loving overtures and invites him 'to come to [his] garden', to 'eat of its choicest fruits'. For the girl this is not the Victorian mother's advice, which went along the lines of 'Lie back and think of England, dear' with its implication that sex is what men do to women under sufferance. There is a mutuality in their lovemaking on their wedding night which continues in the scenes that follow.

The scene ends with the subtle confession of the shepherd that he has indeed 'come to my garden'. He has 'gathered, eaten and drunk' of their wedding night love.

The whole scene is a delicate and nuanced description of the sexual intimacy of those who are newly married. Because it is a part of the Scriptures it tells us that God sets his seal upon such beautiful expressions of human sexuality. It also tells us that there is a high value on virginity and saving sexual intercourse for its proper place within marriage. In the post-modern word of emotivism and 'anything goes', it seems almost quaint to speak of virginity as a good and positive thing. But the truth is it really is good, even the best. The delight of sexual intercourse is to be reserved for those who, before God and others, have entered into the deep commitment of the marriage covenant. The very act of becoming one flesh, and the utter openness and vulnerability which it entails, is not be be cheapened by multiple partners or sex without covenant faithfulness.

A new point of commitment

There are spiritual lessons for us to learn in this part of the Song too. It almost staggers the imagination that God should choose the most intimate of human engagements to picture for us the relationship of Christ and the soul of the believer. Some reading the last few paragraphs may have found difficulty. In earlier commentaries writers sometimes urged the reader not to have any 'carnal' views of the poem. The Song was to be taken only 'spiritually', as if the actual and natural content of the poem (love, sexuality, marriage) was in itself too low for believers to think about. Our feeling is that to 'sanitise' it in that way is to destroy its essential mystery and to deny the God given wonder of human sexuality and depth of sexual relationships between lovers.

Perhaps our difficulties in seeing it in this way are

twofold. In the first place many in the older generations (pre-1960s) were encultured with the idea that sex was in some way or other dirty. Such a notion had great sway in the West from the time of Augustine in the fourth century onwards. That there should be a whole book in the Bible given over to sexual love has been a problem. The solution has been to 'de-carnalise' it and make it speak only of spiritual love. To be sure, it does speak of spiritual love, but under the figure of courtship and marital love.

In the second place, those of us who have grown up post 1960s have largely taken on board the idea that sex is cheap, can be had anywhere under any circumstances and that, in truth, sex is worth little more than self-gratification. For us, that God should use marital love to picture for us relationship with himself might speak to us of something cheap and worth little. There is need for a recovery of the God-given goodness of sexuality and a raising it again to its honoured place as in some way reflecting the image of God ('he made them male and female') and its beauty and mystery in marriage.

God has chosen marital intimacy as a picture of that into which he calls us with himself. The New Testament is replete with the images of the Lord Jesus Christ as the returning bridegroom looking and longing for the consummation of his relationship with his bride, the church. (Mt 9:15; 25:1, 5-6,10; Mk 2:19-20; Lk 5:34-35; Jn 3:29; Rev 18:23; 19:7; 21:2,9; 22:17)

There is to be a wedding feast and a consummation of marriage between God and his people. When that day comes we can only try to imagine the sense of closeness and intimacy the bride will have with her returning bridegroom.

That day can be prefigured for each of us as we draw into ever closer relationship with Jesus. Just as marriage marks a new point of commitment through covenant, in our spiritual lives there will be similar points of commitment. As with the girl in the Song, the Lord will come to us, to draw us further with himself. There will be the proposal of deeper commitment which at times we will reject, feeling that we are not yet ready for God to take us deeper. And yet, by God's grace, there will be times when we are brought to readiness so that when the bridegroom calls we will willingly follow.

One of the strange ways God deals with us is that he will often bring us back to a point of commitment we have faced and balked at previously. It is like coming to a stile on a country ramble, with a field before us we have never entered. Yet we feel the stile is too difficult to climb and so we try to find another way into the field. Having wandered around for some time we find ourselves back at the same stile. This time, however, having meandered for some time, finding only frustration and no other way forward, we eventually climb the stile and enter the new field.

It seems to us that God's ways with us are always brought back to a point of commitment we have turned away from or neglected before.

We faced a situation where we felt God was asking for a certain step of obedience leading to a new commitment. The problem was that for us to take that commitment would be, perhaps, to upset a dear friend. Upsetting our friendship was at that point a stile too difficult to climb. We tried to find another way to the place God was leading us. The search was futile and after some time a similar point of obedience was required, and it still involved the same friendship. This time we chose the way of obedience to a new commitment and a deepening of our relationship with God. As it happened, the friendship was not threatened as we feared it may have been, and the deepening of our relationship with God, in that particular area, was worth the risk. In that instance it felt that God was asking obedience from us regardless of the consequences, which were in his hands all along.

The point we are making is that if the bridegroom comes to us (as he did to the girl in chapter 2), then should we reject his calling he will bring us back to the same point some time later.

This shows his immense patience and grace. Even though we reject him, he is not the kind of lover who will take offence and wash his hands of us. He comes to us again and again and again, always wanting to draw us after him.

A new and deeper commitment is not a negative or difficult thing. For the girl, having responded to her lover and entered into the marriage covenant, she was ushered into a new place of intimacy and delight in her lover. His words of love were ever sweeter, his caresses more intimate and deep. Their mutuality was complete as they lost themselves in one another's arms.

Our relationship with Jesus is much that way. At times a point of commitment may look foreboding. We shy away from it. We think he is asking too much of us. And yet, when by his grace we enter a deeper commitment, the new intimacy into which God brings us is well worth the commitment. In fact, the commitment seems as nothing to that into which we enter.

We heard testimony in the renewal meetings from a pastor's wife who had been a Christian for over 50 years. She and her husband had been at most of the nightly meetings which had at that point been continuing for 17 weeks. She testified to the fact that had she been asked 20 weeks before to make a nightly commitment to renewal meetings that would seldom finish before 11 p.m., and often later, she would have laughed at the thought. Retirement was to be taken at a more leisurely pace! And yet, God had brought her into such a deep, loving relationship with himself that the nightly commitment seemed as no commitment. As she testified she radiated the love of Christ and looked in the peak of health!

Receiving his love

We want to dwell for a while on the words the bridegroom speaks. His words are precious and tell of his immense regard for his bride.

You are altogether beautiful, my love;
    there is no flaw in you.
You have ravished my heart, my sister, my bride,
    you have ravished my heart with a glance of your eyes.

Clearly, to the bridegroom, the bride is the most precious of all people. His affirmations of her are most beautiful and tender. She receives them gladly.

There is a very touching scene in the movie *Three Men and a Little Lady* [1] in which Sylvia (played by Nancy Travis) and Peter (played by Tom Selleck) rehearse together a scene from a play. The play is *Rain Maker* and Selleck plays the part of Starbuck and Travis that of Lizzie.

The scene goes something like this:

> Starbuck: 'Let me ask you Lizzie, are you pretty?'
> Lizzie: 'No I'm plain.'
> Starbuck: 'You don't know you're a woman.'
> Lizzie: 'I am a woman, a plain one.'
> Starbuck: 'Every woman's pretty.'
> Lizzie: 'Not me.'
> Starbuck: 'Now close your eyes Lizzie, close them. Now say "I'm pretty".'
> Lizzie: 'I can't.'
> Starbuck: 'Say it, say it Lizzie.'
> Lizzie: 'I'm pretty.'
> They kiss . . . at first purely as the script dictates, but then as lovers as Peter and Sylvia realise that they truly love each other.

The scene from the movie illustrates for us the truth that many of us (men and women alike) find it difficult to see ourselves as 'pretty' or of any value at all. We can look at others and see in them all manner of qualities and virtues. We can sincerely affirm others and see great good in them. But should anyone say something affirming about us, we have a tendency to reject it. 'Oh, I'm not like that at all'. Like Lizzie in the movie (of the play!) there is that within us which is reluctant to recognise the good.

To the bridegroom in the Song, the bride is perfect. There is no flaw in her. He sees only beauty. As she looks on him he is utterly ravished by the beauty he sees in her. There is every indication that the bride receives these words of loving affirmation. There seems to be no thought of 'What, you can't mean me!'

The astounding truth is that the Lord Jesus Christ looks on us in the same way. He sees no flaw within us. In fact as we look upon him he is ravished by our look of love. Amazing truth! And what's more, he desires to communicate that deep within our spirits. Our hearts are to beat with the fact that our Saviour sees only beauty in us and that as we worship him, his heart is ravished by *our* beauty.

Unfortunately, self-loathing is a common obstacle to growth in love for Jesus. It seems that many of us, because we cannot love ourselves, we find it impossible to receive his love. How could he love us? We are so impure, so dirty, so unclean . . . We are not worthy of love. We are the unlovely. Self-loathing makes it hard for us to receive his love for us.

At times it is portrayed as the zenith of spirituality to have a kind of self-loathing. It appears in what we call a 'miserable worm mentality'. Of course, there is some truth in it. In sin we are loathsome and our deeds of rebellion against God and hatred of him are heinous. But in Christ something new has happened. We have been cleansed of the filth of sin. We have been cleaned, refreshed and reclothed. As God looks upon us now, he only sees the beauty that we are in his Son. In truth there is no flaw in us.

It is an amazing liberating truth. Once we grasp it, it makes way for our bridegroom to speak his words of love and affirmation deep within us without our reacting against his love and rejecting his loving affirmations.

'Lord Jesus, draw me into a deeper relationship with you. Speak your words of love into the depths of my spirit. Grant me revelation to see myself as you see me and to receive your loving affirmations with gladness.'

Note

[1] Touchstone Pictures, Director Emile Ardonlino, 1990.

CHAPTER 9

FURTHER TESTING . . . THE DARK NIGHT OF THE SOUL

My tears have been my food day and night, while people say to me continually, 'Where is your God?' These things I remember, as I pour out my soul: how I went with the throng, and led them in procession to the house of God, with glad shouts and songs of thanksgiving, a multitude keeping festival.

As with a deadly wound in my body, my adversaries taunt me, while they say to me continually, 'Where is your God?' Yet you have rejected us and abased us, and have not gone out with our armies. You made us turn back from the foe, and our enemies have gotten spoil. You have made us like sheep for slaughter, and have scattered us among the nations. You have sold your people for a trifle, demanding no high price for for them. You have made us the taunt of our neighbours, the derision and scorn of those around us. You have made us a byword among the nations, a laughingstock among the peoples. All day long my disgrace is before me, and shame has covered my face at the words of the taunters and revilers, at the sight of the enemy and the avenger. All this has come upon us, yet we have not forgotten you, or been false to your covenant.

If we had forgotten the name of our God, or spread out our hands to a strange god, would not God discover this? For he knows the secrets of the heart. Because of you we are being killed all day long.

From Ps 42–44

The psalmists knew what it was when, seemingly, God turned away from them. When there was sin, and God revealed the nature of that sin, they willingly repented. But there were times when things were bad, when God seemed absent, when they just could not understand why. It was at times a perplexing mystery. Why would God withdraw his presence?

One of the things we appreciate most about the Psalms, and one of God's gifts to us, is that every kind of human emotion finds expression before God. For our purposes, these feelings of the loss of God's presence were both freely expressed and inscripturated for us. There is about the Psalms a reality which, in our experience, is often missing among God's people.

Steve and Anne had been Christians for many years. They had really tried to follow God as well as they knew how. Like most of us, they had from time to time walked in disobedience, but for some time they had been close to God. They had sensed his call to serve him and willingly counted the cost. They gave notice in their respective jobs and pursued the opportunity God had placed before them. It was not a hasty decision. They had weighed it carefully, shared with their spiritual directors, fasted and prayed and, only after some time acted.

Everything went fine until they made their decision. Then everything seemed to go wrong. Doors which had miraculously opened, strangely closed, and both Steve and Anne entered a time of depression. The worst thing of all was that God seemed to disappear. They no longer felt his presence. The Scriptures seemed to close and it was as if there was a lead ceiling between them and heaven. They looked into their hearts to see if there was deliberate sin. They found none. They cried out to God again and again and there was no answer. They remained in this state for about nine months. Spiritually it was very dark.

However, as strangely as they were led into the darkness, the light began to shine again. Only now, both Anne and Steve were less self-confident and more reliant on God. They no longer took his presence for granted, they were less willing to judge others and provide easy answers, and they found a new sensitivity and maturity in spiritual matters.

God used the dark night to bring a new element to their relationship. He used the experience of darkness and all its related feelings to do a deeper work in their hearts.

The ebb and flow of relationship

The Song of Songs is a book with a constant ebb and flow. No sooner are we given the beautiful insights into the marriage of shepherd and shepherdess and its consummation, than we are led again into a period of separation. At this point it presents a puzzle. How can we move from the intimacy of 4:16–5:1 to what appears like the desolation of 5:2ff. Surely, if their marriage was the great climax to their courtship why this period of seeming abandonment again?

In the natural flow of the story we are not told why there is this period of separation. One suggestion might be that it is a dream the bride has, which amounts almost to a nightmare, in which she experiences the awful possibility of the loss of her beloved bridegroom.

Our feeling is that it amounts to a real experience through which their marital love is developed and deepened. Why it is that her beloved is no longer with her we are not told. It remains a mystery to us. In fact, we are content to leave it that way, for there are in every human relationship elements of mystery. In any relationship not all the 'i's can be dotted and not all the 't's can be crossed. It is in the very nature of relationship that it cannot be systematised or fully explained. Those who have lived together for years in the intimacy of marriage certainly know one another in a deeper way than they did in the courtship, and yet there are still hidden and unknown depths to the other. Even in the mystery of 'one flesh' the 'other' remains 'other'. There will not be the 'knowing fully' or 'being fully known' until we enter glory.

It's also totally unrealistic to give the impression that after the wedding service everything is fine. In fact the marriage service and the wedding night are only the beginning. That is the point at which the learning process really begins.

Someone has said, 'You always marry the wrong person!' That's true . . . the very act of getting married changes both people. Learning to relate to another intimately, on a daily basis, is a certain catalyst for change. The give and take of marriage is a wonderful learning experience in how to love another.

In the Song the young bride has much to learn in her ever-deepening relationship with the bridegroom.

> *I slept, but my heart was awake.*
> *Listen! my beloved is knocking.*
>
> 'Open to me, my sister, my love,
>   my dove, my perfect one;
> for my head is wet with dew,
>   my locks with the drops of the night.'
>
> *I had put off my garment;*
>   *how could I put it on again?*
> *I had bathed my feet;*
>   *how could I soil them?*
> *My beloved thrust his hand into the opening,*
>   *and my inmost being yearned for him.*
> *I arose to open to my beloved,*
>   *and my hands dripped with myrrh,*
> *my fingers with liquid myrrh,*
>   *upon the handles of the bolt.*
> *I opened to my beloved,*
>   *but my beloved had turned and was gone.*
> *My soul failed me when he spoke.*
> *I sought him, but did not find him;*
>   *I called him, but he gave no answer.*
> *Making their rounds in the city*
>   *the sentinels found me:*
> *they beat me, they wounded me,*
>   *they took away my mantle,*
>   *those sentinels of the walls.*
> *I adjure you, O daughters of Jerusalem,*
>   *if you find my beloved,*
> *tell him this:*
>   *I am faint with love.*

Song 5:2–8

There are resonances here with the girl's experience of chapter 2, where the beloved called her and she was unwilling to follow. At this point, however, their relationship is much deeper. His words of love now are more full; she is now his 'perfect one'. On her part there is again hesitation, but not as wilful as in chapter 2. There she responded with 'turn my beloved' for she was not going to follow him. Here, it seems there is only a momentary hesitation. She is secure and content, bathed and rested and briefly queries whether to leave her secure and restful place. Yet it is only momentary, little more than a fleeting thought. Even the sight of the bridegroom's hand upon the door moves her deeply. She had learned that lesson of chapter 2. No longer would she ask her beloved to leave without her. Willingly she responds to her beloved. But he has gone and her soul fails her, she is overcome with anxious thoughts and the awful realisation that she is alone.

Again she searches for her lover. This time she is even dreadfully mistreated by the sentinels at Jerusalem. Lost and alone she suffers terribly. It is, in all the Song, the most awful time for the young shepherdess. If the loss of the shepherd's presence in chapter 2 was caused by her unwillingness to follow, in chapter 5 there seems to be no such reason. He has simply withdrawn and neither she, nor we, know why.

Like the psalmist, she would be justified in saying that she had not been disobedient to the covenant, she had been faithful and yet still found herself bereft of the shepherd's presence.

Entering the dark night

Sometimes God withdraws his presence and we don't know why. It happens to all God's people at some time or other. It is not related to any known or conscious sin. It may even arise following a time of immense blessing, intimacy and spiritual growth.

This part part of the Song pictures for us what has sometimes been described as 'the dark night of the soul'. It is a period in spiritual life when, for no apparent reason, God withdraws his felt, beneficent presence and the believer is left with 'naked' faith. If you have never experienced this to date, be thankful. It is not an experience to be sought after, but it is likely that we will all pass through this at least once.

It is a period in a believer's life which can often be handled badly by counsellors, particularly those who have been trained to work to a formula. Indeed, good meaning Christians can cause much damage by pushing too hard in trying to find some sin, some area of blockage or some other reason why God has withdrawn his presence. Some are even threatened by encountering this period of spiritual life in another. Those of us who are more insecure want to surround ourselves with those who are, to all outward intents and purposes, spiritually 'successful'. We need those around us who are 'up' and live the spiritual 'high life'. To be confronted by a godly sister or brother who confesses to having lost the presence of God, and finding no apparent reason for it, can be very threatening.

C.S. Lewis in his brief book *A Grief Observed* [2] vividly describes his feelings when his wife, Joy, died from cancer. It was for Lewis a time of deep sadness. Though the situation was dissimilar to that of the bride in the story, many of the inner feelings are similar. For Lewis, on top of the deep sense of the loss of his wife was the awful feeling that God, too, had withdrawn. Here was a great man of God whose writings were used to help many find God, and yet who passed through the most awful period of loss and separation from God. And yet, our understanding of Lewis is all the richer in knowing that he passed through the darkness and still came into the light. Our appreciation of his depth and spirituality is heightened in knowing that he had passed through the separation and still found faith.

Andy passed through such a time and found people's responses quite interesting. Those with maturity could see the hand of God in God's 'absence', quietly prayed and waited on God. Others came up with the banal encouragements of 'just keep rejoicing', 'walk in the Spirit'. Still others became condemning, and like Job's comforters were desperate to find a reason, probably rooted in some secret sin, or demonic possession, to enable them to feel more secure.

The truth is, at times God withdraws from us that we might learn the depths of the life of faith. When such a time comes, we need to learn to embrace it as a period of deepening our relationship with God.

'The sentinels found me; they beat me, they wounded me'

> In this you rejoice, even if now for a little while you have had to suffer various trials, so that the genuiness of your faith – being more precious than gold that, though perishable, is tested by fire – may be found to result in praise and glory and honour when Jesus Christ is revealed.
>
> 1 Peter 1:6–7

Peter helps us at this point. Though, in the context, Pèter is speaking of persecution by others, his points of application are useful. There is about us that which is more precious than any perishable thing, that is, our faith. But our faith is something which needs to grow, needs to be strengthened, indeed just like gold which perishes, needs to be refined, tested by fire.

The girl's predicament is exacerbated by the persecution she suffers at the hands of the sentinels of Jerusalem. Up to this point in the story she had received mistreatment from her brothers when they made her 'keeper of the vineyards'. She had also endured the mocking of the women of the court of Solomon as they ridiculed her manners and country upbringing. She had not yet faced the severity she receives from the sentinels.

Not only has she lost the presence of the bridegroom, she also suffers persecution. It speaks to us spiritually of not only loosing the sense of Jesus, but also to suffer at the hands of others. Spiritually speaking, the persecution at this point is all the more severe, in that the bridegroom has withdrawn. With his presence, with his comfort and help, we could face anything. Simply knowing that he is with us gives us the courage to face lions. The difficulty at this point is that the girl faces the sentinels alone. She is without the felt presence of the bridegroom. The testing is all the more severe.

We have known periods of 'persecution'. We are, however, a little reluctant to use the term for we are aware that many of our brothers and sisters in closed countries have suffered terribly because of their faith. We have not lost property, nor suffered at the hands of the State, nor have we been called upon to give our lives for Christ. We have, though, known periods of slander and visciousness against us because of our stand for Christ, and for remaining true to where we believed God was leading us.

Strangely, or perhaps not, most of it has been from other believers who have taken it upon themselves to take malicious action or spread half-truths. We have stood before believers who have accused us and maligned us to the church. We have heard from third parties rumours about things we were purported to have done. We have seen believers we led to Christ and baptised turn away from us because of the maliciousness of others in the family of God. Whatever the case, it was always painful. On some of these occasions we were very conscious of the Saviour's presence throughout. In such instances, though there were outward trials, there was always the inner comfort of the Spirit and closeness to Jesus.

There have been times, however, and thankfully very few, when, at a point of the loss of his presence, criticism and slander have been brought. Those times were almost unbearable. During such a time, after a particularly unpleasant telephone conversation with a fellow leader, Andy simply broke down in tears and wept in deep anguish, feeling he could take no more. No sense of God's presence and outward hostility are a weight almost too heavy to bear.

And yet our Saviour faced that in the most extreme form on the cross. Humanity had turned its back upon him, nailing him to the cross. He had voluntarily taken human sinfulness and at that awful point the Father turned from his beloved Son. We will never know what that felt like. But we are called to share in something of his suffering and his dying. Paul calls it; 'the sharing of his sufferings by becoming like him in his death' (Phil 3:10).

There is in this something of mystery and it's the kind of mystery that we would rather do without! Our age is one which shuns any form of suffering as imperfection, and finds no place for it in a developing spirituality. To grow in intimacy with Christ, is, however, to share in his sufferings. To know, in however minor a way, something of what the cross meant for Jesus.

Two dear friends of ours were desperate to have children of their own. Sadly, there were complications. Like many childless couples they passed through infertility treatment and the terrible trauma that the whole process involves. It was a period of deepest sadness. At that time God clearly gave to them the passage we have just considered in Peter. To date, their desire for children has not been fulfilled. It remains a deep longing of their heart and they still suffer the sadness of childlessness. For them it has become a trial through which their faith has been – is being – tested and refined.

Why does God allow these things? The answer must be that in his own sovereign plan there is a purpose in the refining and strengthening of our faith which needs to take place in the absence of his presence.

Returning to Peter a number of things help. First, the dark night is only for a 'little while'. Thankfully, it is not a permanent state. During such a time it may seem never ending, but in truth it is only a little while. God's heart is for us to enjoy his intimacy, not his absence, and yet for a time it may prove necessary.

Secondly, there is purpose in the darkness, even if at the

time we cannot feel it. There is the hidden and secret work of the Spirit of God as he refines the gift that God has given to us. We would prefer that this scene was not within the Song. It would be somehow more palatable if, after the wedding, the bride knew the uninterrupted presence of the bridegroom. It might have made a 'nicer' story, but in truth would not have been at all helpful to us in our growth in intimacy with God. Even in the most godly there will be times when the sense of the absence of God will be almost unbearable and when persecution will compound the difficulty.

Thirdly, with patience we will see that it will, in the end, give glory and praise to God. He will always turn the situation around for his praise and glory.

Notes

[1] Stanley Hauerwas, *A Community of Character*, (University of Notre Dame Press: Notre Dame, 1981), p 172.
[2] C.S. Lewis, *A Grief Observed*, (Faber and Faber: London, 1961).

CHAPTER 10

THE POWER OF WORDS

Jane was having a good day. She felt well and fit. A friend came along and said, 'You're looking very pale. Are you sure you are feeling OK?' Jane responded positively, but the look of concern and pained expression on her friend's face caused her to wonder. She arrived home shortly afterwards and looked in the mirror. Perhaps she wasn't that well after all. The previous sense of well-being began to disappear and a feeling of heaviness descended. Conversely, on another day Jane was feeling somewhat tired. Work had been hard and both in home and church life pressures had mounted leaving her a little drained. While in the supermarket she bumped into a friend she hadn't seen for a few years. After the usual pleasantries, hugs and kisses, the friend took a step backwards, eyed Jane up and down and commented 'Jane, you look so good. Life must be treating you well!' All sense of weariness left as Jane received gladly the words of affirmation and encouragement. The simple truth is that words have a great power for good or ill.

It is fashionable to criticise the 'Word of Faith' school as 'name-it-and-claim-it' or superstitious. We don't want to get into debate at all, but make the comment that there is deep truth in the power of words to affect our lives. The children's rhyme 'Sticks and stones may break my bones, but words will never hurt me!' is unfortunately not true. Words can be wonderfully creative or terribly destructive.

What is your beloved more than another beloved,
    O fairest among women?
What is your beloved more than another beloved,
    that you thus adjure us?

My beloved is all radiant and ruddy,
    distinguished among ten thousand.
His head is the finest gold;
    his locks are wavy,
    black as a raven.
His eyes are like doves
    beside springs of water,
bathed in milk,
    fitly set.
His cheeks are like beds of spices,
    yielding fragrance.
His lips are lilies,
    distilling liquid myrrh.
His arms are rounded gold,
    set with jewels.
His body is ivory work,
    encrusted with sapphires.
His legs are alabaster columns,
    set upon bases of gold.
His appearance is like Lebanon,
    choice as the cedars.
His speech is most sweet,
    and he is altogether desirable.
This is my beloved and this is my friend.
    O daughters of Jerusalem.

Where has your beloved gone,
    O fairest among women?
Which way has your beloved turned,
    that we may seek him with you?

My beloved has gone down to his garden,
    to the beds of spices,
to pasture his flock in the gardens,
    and to gather lilies.
I am my beloved's and my beloved is mine;
    he pastures his flock among lilies.

Song 5:9 – 6:3

The bride in the Song was passing through the most difficult of times. All sense of the bridegroom was missing. She had become desperate in her search for her beloved.

The people of the city question her, realising that her frantic search must be for someone truly special. 'Tell us what's so special about your beloved?'

She responds with a glowing description of the shepherd, in similar tones to those he has used of her and will use again later. She concluded with the confident assertion 'This is my beloved' It is as if in the very act of speaking praise of her lover to others, she finds him again. Their response is to ask where this wonderful person might be. And, wonder of wonders, the Shulammite knows! Her words of love have led her back into the arms of her lover.

In our relationship with Christ and our seeking intimacy with him, words can be very powerful. Inner communion is a precious gift of God. Soaking in his love as the Spirit caresses our spirits while we wait on him is a wonderful experience. But how do we get back to it when, for whatever reason, we lose it?

We have resisted presenting any 'formulas' in our reflections because we believe that in a developing intimate relationship, formulas will not work. But there is a powerful principle which we can learn with profit. Speaking to others of our Saviour often leads us into his presence.

Those who have been preachers know the truth of this. Presenting dull sermons to sleepy congregations can be a wearying task . . . for all concerned! Yet all preachers will have known that point when, as they speak of Christ, trying perhaps inadequately to express something of his wonder and personality, they find themselves carried into his presence. The notes in front of them become unnecessary as the anointing of Spirit and power comes upon them. Irrespective of the congregation in front of them, the preacher is brought to Christ in a personal way. There is an immense privilege in being asked to speak of Jesus Christ. Words are a powerful medium.

A number of biblical strands confirm this for us. The very

instrument of God's creation was the spoken word. Creation came into existence out of nothing as God 'merely' spoke things which were not into being.

Equally, when Paul is explaining the way of salvation in Romans 10, it is confessing with lips, as well as believing in the heart, which leads people to God. He asserts ' . . . one confesses with the mouth and so is saved' (Rom 10:10). Having believed in Jesus, it is often when such belief is verbalised in confessing him that salvation becomes a reality. Confessing with your mouth somehow seems to seal that which God is doing deep inside.

In our struggle with the powers of darkness it is also the spoken word which brings us victory. We win through by actively and boldly confessing our standing in Jesus and our trust in the power of his blood. In one of the visions of Revelation it is made quite clear. Speaking of the devil it says God's people '. . . have conquered him by the blood of the Lamb and by the word of their testimony, for they did not cling to life even in the face of death' (Rev 12:11).

There is something of unfathomable mystery in the power of the words which come from our mouths. We have lost count of the number of times when we have gathered with others to worship feeling somewhat 'out of things'. As we have, by conscious act of will, opened our mouths and given praise to God, despite flat feelings or tiredness or apathy . . . the change is often immediate. Words speaking the truth of God bring us into that truth as an experienced reality.

James, in Peterson's translation, expresses it clearly:

> A word out of your mouth may seem of no account, but it can accomplish nearly anything - or destroy it! . . . By our speech we can ruin a world, turn harmony to chaos, throw mud on a reputation, send the whole world up in smoke and go up in smoke with it, smoke right out of the pit of hell.[1]

We need to learn to speak positive, affirming words which have the power to be creative. Perhaps even more importantly we need to learn to speak words of love concerning our Saviour. We need to know what it is to speak of his grace and his loveliness, to tell others of all that he means to us.

Speaking of him will lead us into deeper intimacy and usher us into his presence. We know it from experience and simply need to practice day by day.

Note

[1] Eugene H. Peterson, *The Message*, (NavPress: Colorado Springs, 1993), p482.

CHAPTER 11

MATURING LOVE

Following the final period of her separation from the bridegroom, we are introduced to an extended period of their love together. There is progression through the three periods of separation and the three periods of being together.

In the first separation (where we enter the book) the shepherdess is characterised by the sense of deep heart longing for the shepherd. She had known his touch, was presently separated from him and deeply desired to know him more. The second separation was more on account of her unwillingness to follow him 'like a gazelle or a young stag on the cleft of the mountains'. The third separation was for her the hardest of all. Their love had grown in such intimacy that to find the bridegroom absent was almost unbearable. The pain of his absence was compounded by mistreatment at the hands of the sentinels of Jerusalem.

Likewise, their periods of being together show a progression. In the first there is the intimate tenderness of courtship love. In the second the consummation of their love upon their wedding night. The third section, which is the longest in the book, begins at 6:4 and continues to the end. It is characterised by a growing maturity and has for us the final lessons of love. It begins with the bridegroom expressing further overtures of love for his bride. It also deals with the remaining self doubt that the bride has with regard to his love.

You are beautiful as Tirzah, my love,
   comely as Jerusalem,
    terrible as an army with banners.
Turn away your eyes from me,
   for they overwhelm me!
Your hair is like a flock of goats,
   moving down the slopes of Gilead.
Your teeth are like a flock of ewes,
   that have come up from the washing;
all of them bear twins,
   and not one among them is bereaved.
Your cheeks are like halves of a pomegranate
   behind your veil.
There are sixty queens and eighty concubines,
   and maidens without number.
My dove, my perfect one, is the only one,
   the darling of her mother,
    flawless to her that bore her.
The maidens saw her and called her happy;
   the queens and concubines also, and they praised her.
'Who is this that looks forth like the dawn,
   fair as the moon, bright as the sun,
    terrible as an army with banners?'

                                   Song 6:4–10

Again the bridegroom's words of love show infinite tenderness and the most amazing appreciation of the bride. He is so much in love with her that the simple look of her eyes overwhelms him! To him she is still 'flawless' and 'perfect'. His description of her demonstrates how deep and intimate is his knowledge of her.

On her part there is still something of incredulity that he should love her so overwhelmingly. She reflects on a previous experience when she was seen by Solomon. It was probably the experience which led Solomon to take her to the royal court.

I went down to the nut orchard,
to look at the blossoms of the valley,
to see whether the vines had budded,
whether the pomegranates were in bloom.
Before I was aware, my fancy set me

in a chariot beside my prince.

Song 6:11–12

The bridegroom responds to her musings by asking her to 'return with him'. It is a call to leave the past and to live in the present: "Return, return, O Shulammite! Return, return, that we may look upon you' (Song 6:13a).

She is, however, still caught in her musings, What is it about her that the shepherd loves her so? What does he see in her? (It is the same incredulity shown by David in Psalm 8:4 'What are human beings that you are mindful of them, mortals that you care for them?') *'Why should you look upon the Shulammite, as upon a dance before two armies'* (Song 6:13b)?

The bridegroom responds by again affirming the bride's beauty in the most intimate speech in the Song.

> How graceful are your feet in sandals,
>   O queenly maiden!
> Your rounded thighs are like jewels,
>   the work of a master hand.
> Your navel is a rounded bowl
>   that never lacks mixed wine.
> Your belly is a heap of wheat,
>   encircled with lilies.
> Your two breasts are like two fawns,
>   twins of a gazelle.
> Your neck is like an ivory tower.
> Your eyes are pools in Heshbon,
>   by the gate of Bath-rabbim.
> Your nose is like a tower of Lebanon,
>   overlooking Damascus.
> Your head crowns you like Carmel,
>   and your flowing locks are like purple;
>   a king is held captive in the tresses.
> How fair and pleasant you are,
>   O loved one, delectable maiden!
> You are stately as a palm tree,
>   and your breasts are like its clusters.
> I say I will climb the palm tree
>   and lay hold of its branches.
> Oh, may your breasts be like clusters of the vine,

and the scent of your breath like apples,
and your kisses like the best wine
that goes down smoothly,
gliding over lips and teeth.

Song 7:1–9

Finally, the bride gives in to the loving affirmations of the bridegroom. It is as if 'the penny drops' and she now realises that he truly does love her above all else. The self-doubt and incredulity give way to her affirmation of their love: '*I am my beloved's, and his desire is for me*' (Song 7:10).

It's quite interesting that most commentaries on the Song concentrate on the early chapters. Those of us who know the book at all tend to be more familiar with the loving expressions in their first encounters than with the latter. In fact, Charles Coates, the Brethren commentator, suggests that the heights of the book are in the first chapter.[1] In the first few verses of the Song the 'goal' to be reached is given in the bride's expressions of love and longing for the bridegroom. For Coates, the rest of the book is mixed and varied in its descriptions. The first part has a purity about it which the rest does not match.

We are taking a different view. Though there is a simplicity and beauty about the opening of the book (and many songs of worship have been written out of it) the book holds for us a picture of the progression of spiritual intimacy with Jesus. In the early scenes the words of the bridegroom are few and most attention is given to the girl's inner state. However, in the latter parts full flow is given to his appreciation of his beloved bride. We are shown in the most beautiful words and figures of speech how much Jesus loves us. How intimately he knows us! How much love he wants to pour into our hearts! With ears to hear there is much that Jesus wants to intimately communicate to our spirits.

This part, then, speaks to us both about ourselves receiving the love of Jesus, and of his ever-deepening words of love in our spirit. It speaks of a deepening and maturing relationship which reaches new expressions of intimacy.

There is, we are sure, more revelation to come from the Song. We have both walked with Jesus for over twenty years. There are things we have seen in the Song recently that we had never seen before. There are experiences that we had only briefly touched upon which are now part of our relationship with him.

In the nature of things, and we believe this will continue for eternity, there will be new appreciations of the love of Jesus. Naturally, this section of the Song contains the most intimate expressions of love. It must speak to us, then, of the most intimate communion with Jesus. We do not believe that we have truly entered into all that this section means. It speaks to us of a deepening relationship with Jesus in which we are more fully known and more fully receive his loving attention.

To be sure we are on the way. Our passion for him is greater now that it was when we began to write this book. He has given us new revelation, sometimes on a daily basis, as we have waited upon him, and prayed for his passion to be revealed in our hearts and spirits.

Nonetheless, there is more to know, more to receive, new heights, new depths. In truth we have hardly yet entered at all. How do we begin to try to communicate the depths of the heart of Jesus for each one of us?

One thing we are sure of is that for the bride, at this point, there is a new appreciation of grace. There is the amazing sense that, though she is not 'worthy', still she is loved. But she struggles somewhat with this.

It is a part of the wonder of being a Christian. How can he love us so much? It is something which we should never take for granted. The bride had, by this point, a long history of intimacy with the bridegroom. She had received much from him and had given much love in response to his. Yet still she wonders how he could love her so. What was there in her that he should love her in such a deep way?

We have often pondered why it is that God should have chosen us. Members of our families, friends who have shared our culture and education, people who have had the same opportunities as we. . . And yet, God has chosen to reveal his love to us. By his Spirit he has softened our spirits, opened the eyes of our hearts and given revelation of his Son. Paul wondered in the same way:

> But when God, who had set me apart before I was born and called me through his grace, was pleased to reveal his Son to me, so that I might proclaim him among the Gentiles, I did not confer with any human being . . .
>
> Galatians 1:15–16

There is something of divine 'transaction' which astounds us when we consider it. He sets us apart before we were born. In time he calls us by grace (none of us deserved or merited his favour). He then reveals his Son in our hearts.

If you have never pondered wonderingly how this could be so, then it is unlikely that you have ever really received it in your heart. The bride had received so much and yet still wondered, 'What do you see in me?' Believers who have received from Jesus again and again are still struck with the immensity of the grace that has been given to them. Charles Wesley expressed it in his hymn, 'And can it be that I should gain an interest in the Saviour's blood. Died he for me who caused his pain, for me who him to death pursued?'

It is a reality to both receive and wonder at. Like most of the truths of the Scriptures there are levels at which we receive it. The new Christian who has been touched by God for the first time, and has newly received the release of forgiveness, knows the truth. Yet it is truth which comes to us again and again in newer more powerful ways. Indeed, the more intimately we know him, the greater the awareness of our own sin and inadequacy, and the greater the wonder at his grace. The truth of grace remains the same. Our appreciation of it grows and deepens.

Note

1 C.A. C. *An Outline of the Song of Songs*, (Stow Hill Bible and Tract Depot: London 1932), pp 5–6.

CHAPTER 12

THE FIRE OF LOVE

In chapter 2 of the Song the shepherd had approached the girl and urged her to follow him. Spring had arrived and it was time for her to come away with him. She declined.

In chapter 7, however, it is the bride who now rejoices in the springtime and urges her bridegroom to come with her. There had thus come a huge turnaround in their relationship. She had grown and matured to the point where his desires had become her desires. What he had wanted, she now wants. In fact, it had become natural to her. She offers her love to the bridegroom in the same way that he had offered his love to her.

> Come, my beloved,
>   let us go forth into the fields
>   and lodge in the villages;
> let us go out early to the vineyards,
>   and see whether the vines have budded,
> whether the grape blossoms have opened
>   and the pomegranates are in bloom.
> There I will give you my love.
> The mandrakes give forth fragrance,
>   and over our doors are all choice fruits,
> new as well as old,
>   which I have laid up for you, O my beloved.

Song 7:11–15.

The next part of the poem is a little difficult to grasp. Here are husband and wife growing together in ever deeper intimacy, and yet she makes a wish that he were like her younger brother. It helps us to understand if we realise that in their culture it was inappropriate for those married to express loving gestures in public.[1] It was, however, acceptable for members of a family to show affection when others were present. It seems, then, that the bride is expressing the desire that she could be at all times affectionate with her shepherd bridegroom, that there would never be a point where they were merely formal with one another.

> O that you were like a brother to me
>   who nursed at my mother's breast!
> If I met you outside, I would kiss you,
>   and no one would despise me.
> I would lead you and bring you
>   into the house of my mother,
>   and into the chamber of the one who bore me.
> I would give you spiced wine to drink,
>   the juice of my pomegranates.
> O that his left hand were under my head,
>   and that his right hand embraced me!
> I adjure you, O daughters of Jerusalem,
>   do not stir up or awaken love
>   until it is ready!

Song 8:1–4

There follows a comment by the residents of their community about the bride: 'Who is that coming up from the wilderness, leaning upon her beloved' (Song 8:5a)? And the girl answers the question, reaching the 'punchline' of the story.

> Under the apple tree I awakened you.
> There your mother was in labour with you;
>   there she who bore you was in labour.
> Set me as a seal upon your heart,
>   as a seal upon your arm;
> for love is strong as death,
>   passion fierce as the grave.
> Its flashes are flashes of fire,
>   a raging flame.
> Many waters cannot quench love,

neither can floods drown it.
If one offered for love
all the wealth of his house,
it would be utterly scorned.

Song 8:5b–7

In their mature love the bride realises that true love is a passionate fire, that is as fierce as death itself. Death, or the grave, is that which none of us can escape. Since the entrance of sin death has been relentless in its pursuit of the human race. The bride says that passionate love is as relentless as death itself. It is a fire which can't be quenched, even by a flood, so fierce it is.

Some years ago, on a ministry trip to the States, we saw the Los Angeles fires on cable TV news. We watched day after day in horror as unstoppable flames spread across beautiful housing developments with incredible speed. We watched as fire fighters tried with all the resources at their command to put out the flames, to no avail. It was heart wrenching as owners of properties wept as they helplessly looked at the flames devouring their homes and land.

A great fire is an awesome thing. The Shulammite had realised what such a fire could do. Not even a flood could quench its flames. But she recognised that she was not speaking of literal flames. She was speaking of the flames of love which both she and her beloved bridegroom shared.

Solomon had tried to win her. He had as good as promised her the wealth of his house. But because of her consuming love for the shepherd, she had scorned Solomon's advances. The fire of love was burning in her heart and nothing would quench it.

If there is one thing which the church of Christ needs to know at present (in fact at any time) it is this kind of passionate all-consuming, unstoppable love. We have been overwhelmed with techniques, programmes, plans and a myriad of other resources. The truth is we desperately need to fall headlong in love with Jesus Christ.

There is much truth in the wisdom which says: 'Hatred

stirs up strife, but love covers all offenses' (Prov 10:12). And, 'Above all, maintain constant love for one another, for love covers a multitude of sins' (1 Pet 4:8). There is that about love which has the power to overcome, to cover up and to win through. Without love, relationships are difficult and fraught. Those who have been married some years know the truth that marriage at times becomes dry. Love wanes somewhat. It is at such times that little irritations become major annoyances. Offhand comments get blown into heated rows. Love is the oil of marriage, smoothing possible points of friction. When love is strong, then much is overlooked, idiosyncrasies are borne with, lapses are covered, because love is strong and purposeful.

Following Jesus when love is weak can be a dry and dreary experience. Little objects become like mountains. Minor setbacks take on unimaginable proportions. When love is strong, we ride the waves with the accomplishment of an expert surfer. But how did we get this love? Where does the passion come from? One thing is clear to us, it is not a matter of work, but of revelation to the soul of the believer. It is grace, not effort. No magic formula. No ten easy steps to knowing the love of God. Captivating our hearts.

For over ten years we have lived in the Tyne Valley in Northumberland. The River Tyne winds its way from Tynemouth and South Shields through Newcastle and on past the smaller villages of the valley, eventually dividing into the rivers North and South Tyne which lose themselves in the hills of Cumbria and Northumberland.

In the lie of the land our home is on an estate of houses half-way up a hill on the southern side of the valley. To get to the main road which joins the cities of Newcastle and Carlisle, it's necessary to go down into the valley, cross the river by a beautiful stone arched bridge and leave the valley on the other side.

It so happens, that on many days in the year, in all seasons, a mist clings to the river. We awake to find the sun already caressing the hills, only to find that for the drive to work we must descend into the mist, with visibility down to only a few dozen metres.

One of the joys of the journey, and one which never ceases to amaze us, is the ascent out of the mist. In a matter of seconds the mist is cleared, the sun is revealed and the cold, damp of the valley gives way to the warmth and spaciousness of the hillside. It amounts to a point of revelation. The sun is always there. We had seen it when we awakened from sleep! But for the time being it is hidden by the densest of mists. In driving out of the mist the sun is revealed in all its beauty and glory. However many times we do the journey it is always a point of awe.

The revelatory instant is not of our making or achieving, it just happens and we are always the more thankful for being alive in such a beautiful world.

In spiritual life there are similarly many points of revelation. They are always God given, always of grace, and always result in utter thankfulness.

To develop the kind of passion for God we have been speaking of in exploring the Song required that kind of revelatory moment when God shows us his own pure, faithful and totally overwhelming love for us. It's in the revelation of his love that our love is sparked into a passionate fire for him. In other words it has its origin in something other than natural zeal and well-meaning. There is the need of supernatural encounter with God.

For some, this may sound like a counsel of despair. If this is all of God, all of grace, all of revelation, then how do we get it? We are surely at the whim of the Almighty who may or may not choose to give us revelation of his love. And if I have not been given the revelation, then I may as well just carry on as before, there is nothing I can do.

There is certainly something here of mystery and we do not want to move into some of the facile Christian 'solutions' to life. In the microwave generation we desire instant answers to all of life's mysteries. There are always, surely, seven or ten steps to instant success!

Almighty God, desiring to be our lover, will not be bound by our easy formulas! The Scriptures do, however, give us clues which will help us in our earnest search for passion. The first is from the lips of the Lord Jesus when the disciples were trying to make some sense of the whole business of praying in Luke 11. We quote from *The Message*, Eugene H. Peterson's imaginative and inspiring translation.[2]

> Ask and you'll get;
> Seek and you'll find;
> Knock and the door will open.

> Don't bargain with God. Be direct. Ask for what you need. This is not a cat-and-mouse, hide-and-seek game we're in. If your little boy asks for a serving of fish, do you scare him with a live snake on his plate? If your little girl asks for an egg, do you trick her with a spider? As bad as you are, you wouldn't think of such a thing - you're at least decent to your own children. And don't you think the Father who conceived you in love will give the Holy Spirit when you ask him?

The simple truth is that God is more willing to bless than we are often willing to receive. We need to have fixed in our minds an understanding of God in which he is not out to trick us, confuse us, punish us, belittle us, or 'teach us a lesson'. His heart is one of complete delight in his children, and more than anything he wants us to receive goodness from himself.

For some of us this is too good to be true. From early childhood our experience of relationship has been that people rarely, if ever, are interested solely in our well-being. There are always strings attached. There is always an other, often hidden, agenda which we find out to our cost. We have trusted people once too often and have had our fingers burnt. Relationships in the end always end up hurting us.

When we enter into relationship with God we bring with us all of our former experiences of relationships. Simply put, we are unable to trust, always looking behind the immediate presentation for the 'catch'. It certainly looks like a juicy worm, but we are convinced it is merely shielding a hook with a nasty barb which will only do us harm. Bringing such an understanding of relationship to God means that we are, in truth, unwilling to trust him fully.

Jesus, surely, knew that is the case for many of us. He taps into our fears by appealing to our own natural parental goodness. Even though we are capable of all manner of sins, towards our own children we have an innate love and care. And now God is our Father! He's got to be better then we are!

The clue we are seeking in moving towards passion for God, is to believe that God desires to bring us there even more than we do. If we ask, he will give it. If we ask for the fire of love, God will give it. It is a question of bringing our thinking about him into line with the Scriptures, and then diligently seeking him.

A further clue is that grace is given to the humble. The fire of love is not for those who are proud or who believe they have something to offer to God of themselves. James is very clear.

> Or do you suppose that it is for nothing that the scripture says, 'God yearns jealously for the spirit that he has made to dwell in us'? But he gives all the more grace; therefore it says, 'God opposes the proud, but gives grace to the humble.'
>
> James 4:5–6

Verse 5 is notoriously difficult, both to translate and interpret. No two translations give the same rendering. Translators and commentators differ as to whether the 'jealousy' belongs to the human spirit or to God. If the NRSV is correct, then we are faced with a God who is jealous over his people. Eugene Peterson paraphrases it 'he's a fiercely jealous lover'. Interestingly Deuteronomy links fire and jealousy: 'For the Lord your God is a devouring fire, a jealous God' (Deut 4:25).

The truth is that God has an intense longing for the love of his people, to such an extent that the analogy of jealousy is used to depict him. But his jealousy is not impotent as, perhaps, a jilted lover might be. His longing for the hearts of his people has prompted him to pour out grace upon those he longs for.

To receive that grace there is the simple matter of humility. Those with humble hearts will find grace. The fire of God will burn in their hearts and they will discover a consuming passion for the Son of God. Grace and humility go together.

Significantly, as God moves in the power of the Spirit, one of the first fruits of his move is to bring a humbling to proud hearts. Many leaders of churches in the Autumn of 1994 found themselves humbled both before God and before the people they led.

On Friday, 2nd September 1994, a group of some 500 young people experienced the power of God in a remarkable way. They were attending a camp for teens in the grounds of a castle in County Durham. As they met in the 'big tent' the wind of the Spirit blew powerfully and around 400 of them found themselves unaccountably falling to the ground.

Our two teenage sons were part of that gathering, and we listened eagerly on Saturday as we shared a 'bag of chips' on the grass outside their tent. We decided to stay through for the evening meeting, awestruck by the power of God we evidently saw all around us in the lives of young people.

The message that night was a simple message of three points, the final one being that if there were any unconfessed sins, people were to leave their seats, come forward and meet with God. It happened that God had spoken clearly to Andy during the teaching and the invitation confirmed the voice of God. But this was a young people's meeting. These were all kids! Surely, God didn't mean the adult, more mature types, leaders even, to stand with the teenagers at the front. The thought came, 'Sort it out afterwards with one of the pastors who you know well . . . leaders together and all that!'

God wouldn't allow it. After 21 years as a Christian and 13

as a pastor, Andy found himself standing at the front of a tent meeting, surrounded by young people, confessing his sins with the rest of them. To cap it all the young person on the 'ministry team' who came to counsel and pray for him was a young person to whom Andy had ministered a number of times in different contexts!

The whole experience was deeply humbling. In God's ways there is a levelling of all of us before him. Proud hearts are incompatible with the presence of God, and many of us have become proud . . . proud in our achievements, proud in our ministries, proud of our successful churches, proud in our knowledge and theology, proud in our experiences.

If we are serious in our desire to know the passionate love of the Father for the Son, then there will be a humbling. God will not humiliate us. That is never his agenda. But humbling there is to be, and having been humbled we will receive abundant grace and the fire of God will burn inside us instead of our natural pride.

Notes

[1] See S. Craig Glickman, *A song for Lovers* (Inter Varsity Press: Downers Grove, 1980), pp 89ff.
[2] Eugene H. Peterson, *The Message* (NavPress: Colorado Springs, 1993), pp 146–147.

CHAPTER 13

FAITHFUL TO THE END

We have a little sister,
   and she has no breasts.
What shall we do for our sister,
   on the day when she is spoken for?

If she is a wall,
   we will build upon her a battlement of silver;
but if she is a door
   we will enclose her with boards of cedar.

I was a wall,
   and my breasts were like towers;
then I was in his eyes
   as one who brings peace.
Solomon had a vineyard at Baal-hamon;
   he entrusted the vineyard to keepers;
   each one was to bring for its fruit a thousand pieces of silver.
My vineyard, my very own, is for myself;
   you, O Solomon, may have the thousand,
   and the keepers of the fruit two hundred!

O you who dwell in the gardens,
   my companions are listening for your voice;
   let me hear it.

Make haste, my beloved,
   and be like a gazelle
or a young stag
   upon the mountains of spices!

Song 8:8–14

It is not always easy to discern who the speakers are in the Song. Following the Amplified Bible, we are taking the first part of this section to be words spoken by the brothers of the Shulammite, the companions of the shepherd, expressed to her when she was young, and now brought to remembrance.

Like all good brothers they had been concerned with the well-being of the young girl and were jealous to protect her. Of course, we are given hints in the first chapter that their care was not always the best in making her the keeper of the vineyards. Nevertheless, at this point there is a reflection on their apprehension for her chastity. Their reference to a 'wall' seems to speak of their hope that, as the girl grew towards maturity, she would remain chaste. In speaking of a 'door', they express a fear that she might become morally loose, for a door is easily opened.

Her response in mature reflection (she is now married to the shepherd) is to say that they need not have worried. She had remained chaste until her marriage. She had grown to maturity (in the reference to her breasts as towers) but had remained as a wall (chaste). She continues by affirming that though Solomon had many vineyards (a veiled reference to the women of his harem), she had remained pure and had not given in to his overtures and attentions. Her vineyards had remained her own.

She finally calls upon her beloved bridegroom to take her away with him. We are left with the great sense of the triumph of faithful love against all the odds. The shepherdess had been faithful to her one true love to the very end.

At the end of the Song we are given a beautiful reflection on faithfulness. Our testimony is that we have known the utter faithfulness of God. Looking back on well over 20 years as believers we can say with no shadow of doubt that God has remained faithful to us. Every promise he had made, and our hearts have received, he has fulfilled. Even when we have passed through dark times, even the blackest periods, looking back our God was faithful.

On the morning that we were writing this chapter we

received a letter from Fred, a dear man who we met as a 'friend of a friend'. Fred had written his testimony at our request as we were anxious to 'test the fruit' of the renewal which had swept many parts of the church in 1994. As we read Fred's words we were struck by the wonderful affirmation of faithfulness which his letter portrayed,

He tells of the faithfulness of his adopted parents who took him as a young boy, prayed for him and brought him up in a 'good evangelical home'. When Fred was later converted to Christ, his adopted father received the news with tears of joy and thankfulness.

Fred joined the Navy and later the Royal Marines. He tells of the faithfulness of a young Christian man he had shared a room with in Plymouth whose 'whole life told everyone he met that there was something different about him'. It was in August 1975 that Fred was led to Christ at 3.00 am through a part-time missionary who stayed up all night with him answering his many questions about Jesus.

For the next few years Fred's life followed the ups and downs of many new Christians. In the Services he was often cut off from Christian fellowship and in his own words he 'slowly died, little by little'.

God, however, was faithful and in 1981 on a tour of duty in Northern Ireland Fred began following Jesus again more closely.

The following year Fred's life fell apart. He was badly injured in the Falklands Conflict and began the struggle to walk again with constant pain and many operations which dogged his life from then on.

From then until October 1994 Fred was in daily and constant pain. However, having heard that God was pouring out blessing he made the trip from Arbroath in Scotland to Sunderland for a long weekend which he describes as 'now infamous!'

On the Friday of that weekend God firstly healed some old inner wounds and dealt with some bad episodes of his life. On the Saturday, in response to an invitation from the front, Fred acknowledged to God that he was in pain and needed healing. There and then with no human instrumentation (no-one prayed for Fred directly) he was healed as he fell to his knees before God.

From that moment until now Fred has been without pain and has taken no medication. God had in utmost faithfulness healed his child.

On reading Fred's testimony we were thrilled at the faithfulness of God. Throughout all Fred's ups and downs God had remained constant in them all.

Undoubtedly, God is faithful. But these final verses of the Song speak not about the shepherd's faithfulness. It is taken as a 'given' that he has been faithful. Any lack of fidelity on his part towards the girl is never even hinted at. She, on the other hand, had passed through a number of circumstances when her faithfulness was tested.

In chapter 1 she is found in the harem of Solomon with all its attractions and distractions from the love of the shepherd. In chapter 2 there is the beginning of a hint that the court of Solomon had begun to attract her. When the shepherd calls her away with him she hesitates and in the end refuses, at that moment, to follow. In the further test of chapter 5 her hesitation is less and her willingness greater. The more intimate and triumphant scenes of the last few chapters show that she had grown in her faithfulness.

It raises for us a point of serious self-examination. 'Lord, you have been utterly faithful to me. You have never let me down. But Lord, I am not confident of my faithfulness to you'.

The parable of the talents has those wonderful words, spoken by the master to the servants: 'His lord said to him, "Well done, good and faithful servant; you were faithful over a few things, I will make you ruler over many things. Enter into the joy of your lord" ' (Mt 25:23, NKJV).

More than anything we want our Lord to say the same things to us in that final day. 'Jane, you have been faithful. Andy you have been faithful . . . enter my joy'.

When we break our faithfulness

It can be a worry. If you are serious about God and honest with yourself, you know times when you have not been faithful. There have been points of walking away from some issue of obedience. There have been recurring thoughts and patterns of behaviour which are dishonouring to the bridegroom. There have been points of spiritual adultery. There is the realisation of having failed, of having grieved his heart. What can we do?

The prophet Hosea gives great insight into the way God relates to his people as husband to wife. Chapter 2 of the prophecy is sober reading. Though God had been totally faithful to Israel and had been to her as a wonderful husband, Israel had committed adultery. She had looked to other gods and 'played the whore'. Reading the story you cannot help feel God's pain and anger. It is as if his unfaithful people had broken his heart. And yet his response is utterly amazing.

> Therefore, I will now allure her, and bring her into the wilderness, and speak tenderly to her . . . And I will take you for my wife forever; I will take you for my wife in righteousness and in justice, in steadfast love, and in mercy. I will take you for my wife in faithfulness; and you shall know the LORD.
>
> Hosea 2:14, 19–20

The truth of God is amazing: His faithfulness always overshadows and covers our faithlessness.

Naturally, this is a deeply sensitive area. We have known couples where one partner has been unfaithful to the other and an 'affair' ensues. With some there has been forgiveness when the unfaithfulness is uncovered, and a marriage saved. With others we have seen marriages fall apart as the wronged partner has struggled with the awful truth of betrayal.

Whatever the outcome, there is always a terrible amount of pain for all parties concerned. The one wronged feels trust has gone, while often, the one who slipped into infidelity faces an almost overwhelming sense of failure and guilt at having betrayed the one they love the most.

It is no less true in the spiritual realm. When we become aware that we have failed our Saviour and flirted with others there will always be a sense of shame. How could we look into his eyes again having hurt him so badly? Confessing our sin we can always shelter in this faithfulness, knowing that he has revealed himself to be a husband who will never turn away from his wife. It is a truth of amazing implications.

CHAPTER 14

DEVELOPING INTIMACY

Don't be passive about acquiring passion for the Son of God. Make it the focus of your life. Put your eyes on the Son of God and leave them there (Heb 12:2), and you will find yourself becoming like him. You will find yourself falling in love with him as you ask God day after day to consume you with passion for his glorious Son.[1]

The meeting had reached the point where the leader explained to the people how the Spirit of God had been poured out, and how, as a consequence, we had been meeting every night of the week (except Monday) since the summer. Leading on this occasion was a dear man who many hundreds still think of as their 'pastor'. Herbert Harrison had been founder and senior pastor of Bethshan Christian Centre in Newcastle-upon-Tyne, who, with his wife Mary, had served God for 38 years. Many people of all denominations in the North East of England looked upon Herbert as a 'senior statesman' among Christians. In God's goodness Herbert and Mary, now in retirement, were members of Sunderland Christian Centre, where the Spirit of God moved powerfully in 1994.

As Herbert gave his explanation to the hundreds gathered to seek God, the Spirit fell forcefully on Andy. The physical phenomena were so powerful as to literally double him up where he sat. To those observing it looked for all the world that Andy had been taken with severe stomach cramps! At these meetings, phenomena of this sort were regularly seen and the meeting proceeded as 'normal'.

Inside God gave a powerful revelation. It was to the effect that as the Father loved the Son . . . 'You are my beloved Son, in you I am well pleased' . . . so we are to love him. That God was putting *his* passion for Jesus upon the hearts of his people.

This was new revelation to Andy. Loving Jesus had been about stirring up our love . . . trying, striving to love him more. God was now showing that the most perfect love, in fact his love, was what he required. And his love was a wonderful gift, a matter of grace. God was pouring his love into our hearts that we might return it in love for the Son of God.

Some time later it was almost a shock to find that Jack Deere had already written the same revelation in his book *Surprised by the Power of the Spirit*. He expressed it in these words: '*He [Jesus] wanted his disciples to love him like his heavenly Father loves him*. He wanted the love that his Father has for him to be in his disciples'.[2]

It seems clear that on God's agenda is a radical all-consuming love for his Son Jesus. Indeed, it has always been God's agenda from all eternity. Jesus explains it to us in his 'High Priestly Prayer' of John 17. In this passage, perhaps above all others, we are given an insight into eternity from the lips of the Son of God himself. Father and Son were intimately involved with one another, being forever in the other's presence (verse 5a); the Son had shared eternal glory with his Father (verse 5b); all that the Son had, had been given to him by the Father (verse 7); the Father had given his words to the Son (verse 8); they mutually share all that is theirs (verse 10); the Father has given his name to the Son (verse 11a); Father and Son are one (verse 11b).

The love relationship of Father and Son is a deep and eternal mystery. Indeed, the Trinity has always been a great truth to be received by faith, rather than analysed with the mind.

What is astounding in John 17 is that Jesus prays to the Father to receive believers into that same kind of relationship: 'As you, Father, are in me and I am in you, may they also be in us, so that the world may believe that you have sent me . . . I in them and you in me . . . so that the love with which you have loved me may be in them, and I in them' (John 17:21, 23, 26).

On his last night on earth the Son of God prayed for the intimate relationship of Father and Son to be their own. Uppermost in the heart of Jesus was that those who believed in him would share that same depth of communication and intimacy with himself that he and his Father had shared for all eternity.

We have, in the past, to a great extent replaced that heart's desire of Jesus with external things. We have been concerned with mere teaching, with programmes, with ministries, with evangelism, with outward holiness . . . all good things. But we have missed the best. The best is an intimate relationship with Jesus Christ, an all-consuming passion out of which all else flows. The words of Jesus himself are salutary:

> 'Not everyone who says to me, 'Lord, Lord,' will enter the kingdom of heaven, but only the one who does the will of my Father in heaven. On that day many will say to me, 'Lord, Lord, did we not prophesy in your name, and cast out demons in your name, and do many deeds of power in your name?' Then I will declare to them, 'I never knew you; go away from me, you evildoers.'
>
> Matthew 7:21–23

It is not the level of 'doing' that is required of us. It is the level of 'being'. There is nothing wrong with prophecy, deliverance and works of power. Indeed, God has graciously restored these to the church. However, the warning is clear. These things are not considered by Jesus as fruit. Fruit is rather the hearts of disciples changed, renewed and fired with passion for him.

Intimacy and fruit

Eugene Peterson catches the heart of the message of Jesus about the vine in these words: 'I am the Vine, you are the branches. When you're joined with me and I with you, the relation intimate and organic, the harvest is sure and abundant.'[3]

We are convinced that it is primarily intimacy with Jesus which produces fruit pleasing to the Father. In the beginning, the first command to the newly created man and woman was for them to be fruitful. Many newly married couples, after a period of being 'wrapped up in each other', desire the fruitfulness of producing children. That was certainly our experience. There is the inward desire, born of deep love, to reproduce, to be fruitful.

In our recent experience of spiritual refreshing, when people have fallen radically and totally in love with Christ, we have seen the most amazing fruitfulness. The desire to become fruitful follows naturally from a relationship of closeness to Jesus. Those whose hearts have been renewed in the power of the Spirit of God long to see many others brought into the kingdom of God.

When the Spirit came powerfully to the North East of England, from the first it was the concern of those leading meetings to hear the stories of those who were being touched. Though outward manifestations were plenty, those interviewed were always asked about the fruit being produced in their lives. Jokingly, interviewers more than once referred to themselves as 'fruit inspectors'.

This desire for fruit is found within the Song, particularly towards the end when the Shulammite has grown in maturity.

In chapter 3:4, in the reference to 'the chamber of her that conceived me', there is a veiled reference to her desire to produce children. There is a similar reference in 8:5 when she says, 'There your mother was in labour with you; there she who bore you was in labour.'

Some commentators consider the speech of 8:8ff to be

that of the bride herself rather than her brothers or the shepherd's companions. Having reached maturity she thinks of those who, like her, were once merely children. There is a strong feeling of protectiveness, of longing to 'parent' the little sister, which in itself is a fruit of the intimacy of mature relationship with the bridegroom.

These clearly lead us to the conclusion that as we grow in intimacy with the Lord, we too will have a deep heart commitment for others. There will be the desire to produce fruit and to care for those who are merely infants in Christ.

The Song as our guide

If God's agenda is to put his love for Jesus upon our hearts, then we believe that the Song of Songs will be our best guide. As we have spent time with this little book, God has been gracious in giving new revelations and insights to us. Many of them we have tried to share in this book. Some of them we are pondering in our hearts. Some are too deep and personal even to write down for others' eyes. We are convinced that if any of us dwell in the Song for any length of time, pondering it, meditating upon it, feeding our spirits with its words of love, then we will develop greater intimacy with him.

In our interpretation we have painted with broad strokes. There were places where we could have moved into the detail of allegory as God spoke to us concerning himself. But we resisted in the belief that many such 'words' will be given to any who dwell upon this book. Many of those words will be personal and intimate as God pours his love into your heart. Many will be 'words of the moment' in which God addresses a particular issue in your life.

Stories have immense influence in all cultures of the world. We hope that in the way we have told the story of purity and beauty of the love of shepherd and shepherdess, that you will have found many resonances in your life with Jesus. Some of the experiences we have recounted will be strange to you. You may yet have to walk that way. Doubtless, there are parts of your story which we need to hear, revelations which you have that we have yet to see. God will lead us in his way and his time.

Notes

[1] Jack Deere, *Surprised by the Power of the Spirit*, (Kingsway: Eastbourne, 1994), p 201.
[2] *Ibid*, p 200.
[3] Eugene H. Peterson, *The Message* (Nav Press: Colorado Springs, 1993), p 221.

APPENDIX A
ANALYSIS

The Song of Songs is a beautiful poem of love. It has been interpreted in many different ways. Jews and Christians alike have found within it allegories and types of God's relationship to his people. For Jews between Yahweh and Israel; for Christians between Christ and the church, or else Christ and the individual believer. Others have found the Song to be a collection of love poems with no apparent connection between them. Most recently, some scholars have taken the poem as a biblical affirmation of the rightness and beauty of married sexual love.

The analysis presented here is based upon that of Dr. E.W. Bullinger in his *Companion Bible* and which sees the Song as a touching love story between a beautiful young girl and her shepherd lover. One day the girl, unwittingly, is seen by King Solomon, who immediately desires her, and takes her to his royal tents. The girl is ridiculed by the other court ladies. Solomon tries, through flattery and the promise of riches, to win her affection. The girl will have none of it. She thinks constantly about and speaks frequently of her shepherd lover. The shepherd lover in his turn urges the girl to follow him that their love may be consummated in marriage. The poem tells of their intimacy together and the testing of their love. In the course of time they are in fact married and their love continues to grow and mature. The story ends with the affirmation that true love conquers all.

The authorship of the book has traditionally belonged to Solomon, who under guidance of the Spirit wrote the poem as a testimony to the purity and faithfulness of true love between a man and woman. As such it stands as an example and extended illustration for us of the faithful love that our heavenly shepherd lover has for us, and also as a demonstration of the faithfulness we are to have for our shepherd. Our faithfulness to him must be above all else, and must stand against the temptations and attractions of the world and the corruption of our own nature.

The analysis which follows is in order to help with the 'natural' sense of the poem, recognising that it is quite difficult to always discern who is speaking in the poem. Spiritual interpretation is left for the chapters of the book.

First Section 1:1–11
Introduction

The girl who has been separated from her beloved shepherd has been taken to the court of Solomon. She expresses the deep longing of her heart for her shepherd lover.

- 1:1 Solomon's most beautiful song.
  - 1:2–4 The girl remembers her beloved shepherd.
    - 1:5–6 The girl speaks to the court ladies who look down upon her.
  - 1:7 The girl again speaks with longing of her shepherd.
    - 1:8 The court ladies answer the girl.
- 1:9–11 Solomon speaks his admiration of the girl.

Second Section 1:12 – 2:7
The girl and her beloved shepherd are together

At some point, while Solomon is resting, the shepherd and shepherdess renew their love.
  - 1:12–14 While Solomon is at his table the girl and the shepherd meet. She renews her vows of love.
    - 1:15 The shepherd renews his love for the girl.

- 1:16–2:1 The girl to the shepherd.
  - 2:2 The shepherd to the girl.
- 2:3–7 The girl to the shepherd.

Third Section 2:8 – 3:5
The girl and the shepherd are apart.

The shepherd urges the girl to come away with him, that their love may be consummated. The girl hesitates, the shepherd leaves and she searches for him in desperation.

- 2:8–14 At a later time when the shepherd has gone . . . The girl tells the court ladies of her shepherd lover.
  - 2:15 She remembers the words of her brother.
- 2:16–17 The girl tells the court ladies how she is waiting for her beloved.
  - 3:1–3 And how after having a troubled night's sleep she rose to try to find her beloved and was hindered by the watchmen.
- 3:4 She then tells the court ladies how she found her beloved.
  - 3:5 She implores the court ladies not to hinder her love.

Fourth Section 3:6 – 5:1
The girl and the shepherd are together.

The story is interrupted by the arrival of Solomon with his stately retinue to Jerusalem. It presents a final challenge to the love of the Shulammite. The shepherd proposes in loving affirmations of the girl. She responds and they are married.

- 3:6–11 The inhabitants of Jerusalem remark on the coming of Solomon in his splendour and wealth to Jerusalem. It amounts to the greatest temptation for the young girl.
  - 4:1–5 The shepherd, now as the bridegroom, speaks words of love to his bride.

- 4:6 The girl, now as the bride, promises to return with him.
  - 4:7–15 The bridegroom speaks words of love on their wedding night.
    - 4:16 The bride declares that all she has is for his pleasure.
  - 5:1a The bridegroom suitably responds.
- 5:1b The daughters of Jerusalem encourage them in their love.

Fifth Section 5:2 – 8:4
The girl and the shepherd are apart.

Even after their marriage love has to grow and is challenged again. There is a separation for reasons which we are not told. The Shulammite again longs for her lover. She is speaking to others about her sense of loss.

- 5:2–8 Again the girl speaks to the inhabitants of Jerusalem about the sense of loss of her beloved.
  - 5:9 The people are amazed at her love and inquire further.
- 5:10–16 The girl further describes her beloved.
  - 6:1 The people enquire again.
  - 6:2–3 The girl answers.

Sixth Section 6:4 – 8:14
The conclusion of the story

The Shulammite and shepherd are together. Their love goes to even greater depths. She reflects on her experience.

- 6:4–10 The shepherd speaks words of love.
  - 6:11–12 The girl reflects on how her meeting with Solomon was unintentional.
- 6:13a The shepherd wants her to 'return' with him, to leave the past.
  - 6:13b Reflecting again, the girl ponders 'What do you see in me?'
- 7:1–9 The shepherd renews his love.

- 7:10–8:4 The girl finally confesses her love.
- 8:5a The companions of the shepherd see them returning to the countryside.
  - 8:5b–7 The girl renews her vows again to the shepherd. The 'punchline' of the whole story is in verses 6–7. However much Solomon had, even if he gave everything he owned, he could not win the love of the girl. She was faithful to her shepherd lover.
- 8:8–9 The brothers of the girl reflect on their sister's experience. 'If she is a wall (ie virtuous) we will adorn her. If she is a door (open to any, immoral) we will shut her up.'
  - 8:10–12 The girl expresses her virtue . . . she did not give in to Solomon's advances but has kept herself.
- 8:13 The shepherd wants her to tell him the whole story.
  - 8:14 The girl finally confesses again her love for him.

APPENDIX B

FURTHER NOTES ON
INTERPRETATION

In our reflections on the Song of Songs we have deliberately steered clear of questions relating to the difficulties in the text and its translation from Hebrew to English, and those of historico-critical interpretation. Such questions are dealt with adequately in a number of works on the Song and these reflections were never intended to be a commentary or strictly speaking an exegesis of the poem.

However, that is not to say that such questions are irrelevant and we wanted to include these brief notes to give a more scholarly reflection on the method we have adopted, and some insight to our underlying thinking. We believe what has preceded stands alone, but some readers may wish to consider the interpretative principles we have adopted. There are basically two hermeneutical clues we have used as guidelines.

Reader response

Since the Reformation, the dominant school of interpreting the Scriptures has been the historico-critical method. This form of interpretation sees the main question as trying to discern the history of the text and to discover the meaning in its original setting. Once that interpretation is found, some form of application to the present is made.

At the time of the Reformation this was to get to the 'literal sense' of the text. This was not, as in some modern fundamentalism, the idea that every statement was to be taken 'literally', but that there was a first and prior understanding of the text in the author's mind. Indeed, that meaning was the one readers were to strive for, and having found it, to guard it against other interpretations. The Reformers reacted in part to the over-allegorisation and spiritualisation of the Bible which had taken place in the Middle Ages.

In later centuries the historico-critical method developed utilising current literary techniques, and scholars became concerned with discovering how the texts came to be written. Questions as to the various sources which composed a text, the form the text was originally in, what principles the editor of the text used etc., became the major issues of interpretation.

We are oversimplifying the long historical process, but the result has been in some ways unfortunate. We do not want to suggest that the historico-critical task is a blind alley, and there is clearly a need for such diligent scholarship. However, the technical skills needed to carry out the critical process has made the Scriptures somewhat inaccessible to the non-theologian. Indeed, the whole Protestant tradition of relying on theologically trained pastors to interpret the Scriptures to the people has reinforced the idea that the Bible can only be handled by experts.

More recently, some scholars have come to a realisation that the Scriptures are not the sole property of the academic theologians or the clergy, and that the average believer has, over all the centuries, found immense benefit from simply reading and allowing the Scriptures to directly address them. This new emphasis (that is, new in an academic sense) has taken place alongside developments in literary criticism given the generic title 'reader response theories'. Simply put, it is a legitimate exercise to take a finished text (in our case the Song of Songs), to spend time with it, and to allow the text to address the reader irrespective of the critical questions surrounding the text. The text is taken as it stands in its finished and translated whole and the reader makes his or her response to the text.

That response may or may not be adequate and needs to be judged by other criteria. In Christian terms, an adequate response would be one which conforms to God's revelation in Jesus and which brings glory to the Father. We might also want to say that a basic Christian orthodoxy would be part of the criteria for judging a response.

Of course, as believers, we also understand that the work of interpretation is not merely a natural thing. There is the work of the Holy Spirit in the whole process of reading and responding. As we read the Scriptures, asking for God's guidance, we believe that the Spirit guides us into truth.

In this way, it is likely that there will be, over time, many differing interpretations of a book like the Song of Songs, arising out of the differing contexts that readers find themselves in. It's for that reason that reflections on the Song often come during times of spiritual awakening; its basic message of a love relationship fits so well with the believer's experience in such a time of spiritual outpouring.

These reflections, then, are our response to the Song of Songs arising from a particular context: that of experiencing an outpouring of God's blessing.

Narrative theology

Our second hermeneutical clue is that of narrative theology. Again, the term is somewhat vague but stands for a way of looking at the text through the means of story. We cannot, in these brief notes, defend the method (that belongs to other works), but simply want to assert that for us it is a useful way of interpreting the Scriptures.

Briefly, the Bible is a book of stories, chiefly the stories of the people of Israel and Jesus. It is through these principal stories, and countless other minor narratives, that God has chosen to reveal himself. The Christian church has continued over the centuries to re-tell the stories of Israel and

Jesus and to find itself in the ongoing unfolding of the narrative of God in the world through the Holy Spirit.

This has been experienced again and again when the most powerful presentations of the gospel are those which are intertwined with the life of a person who has been radically affected by Jesus. Then Christianity is not seen as mere theory, but as a deep reality as it has affected the story of someone to whom we can relate.

In interpreting the Song we have sought to develop a narrative framework to the book. We are aware that some scholars think such a 'narrative plot' is an unnecessary imposition on what they believe to be a number of unconnected and repeated short poems about human sexuality and marital love. We are aware, too, that there are many such 'narratives' given for the Song of Songs. We are not claiming, then, that the way we have told the story of shepherd and shepherdess is the only way to tell the story. We are merely suggesting that it is one which we believe holds a certain consistency and which has fed us spiritually as we have used it in reading the Song.

We have also used narrative theology in that we have weaved within the telling of the story of the two lovers our own story of our relationship with God. In doing so we hope that readers have been enabled to find themselves in the story. 'Yes, it was a bit like that for me!' is a response that we hope many will find as they have delved into the book.

We are aware that there are many questions unanswered about the Song of Songs and new depths yet to be tapped. At the end of the day, if we have helped any to move towards a deeper relationship with their Saviour, our desire will have been fulfilled.

SELECTED BOOKS TO
HELP FURTHER

**Books on the Song of Songs as the believer's
relationship with Christ:**

Watchman Nee. *The Song of Songs*, Christian Literature
Crusade: London, 1965.
C.A.C. [Coates]. *An Outline of the Song of Songs*, Stow Hill
Bible and Tract Depot: London, 1933.
Hudson Taylor. *Union and Communion*, Overseas Missionary
Fellowship: London 1894, last printed 1970.
Jesse Penn-Lewis. *Thy Hidden Ones*, The Overcomer Litera-
ture Trust: Poole, n.d.
George Burrows. *The Song of Solomon*, first published 1853,
Banner of Truth Trust: Edinburgh, 1958.

**Books which see the Song as a representation of
marital love at its best:**

S. Craig Glickman. *A Song for Lovers*, InterVarsity Press:
Downers Grove, 1980.
Tom Gledhill, *The Message of the Song of Songs*, IVP: Leicester, 1994.
(This book is an up-to-date exposition of the Song and deals
with many of the critical questions which our reflections
have left untouched.)

Two books which have excellent comments on developing intimacy with Jesus:

Jack Deere. *Surprised by the Power of the Spirit*, Zondervan: Grand Rapids, 1993; Kingsway: Eastbourne, 1994, chapters 13–14.
Mike Bickle. *Passion for Jesus*, Kingsway: Eastbourne, 1994.